WHAT PEOPLE ARE SAYING...

In an age when marriage is often scoffed at as 'irrelevant', old fashioned and 'so 1979'!! I, for one, stand proudly as an advocate for it! Married for over 46 years to the same man (Phil Pringle), as each year passes, he's still my gorgeous, kind, creative boyfriend whom I fell in love with, (and married) so long ago! Except now we are middle aged companions in this great big life- parents to three adult children and "G-Parents" to four "G-Babies" (so far!!). Marriage is to be celebrated, enjoyed and honoured - and I will endorse any book which advocates this sacred commitment. Called to Love is such a book! Enjoy the read friends.

Pastor Chris Pringle

C3 Church Oxford Falls, Sydney

No other time in history is humanity more engaged with each other, and simultaneously, disengaged. The paradox of this time is that we are living in a global economy with people feeling more isolated and more alone than ever before. It's easy to hide our uniqueness (and our inadequacies) behind social media posts, apps that photoshop us (and our lives) into that perfect person, couple, family, or business. And while there is a part of us that understands this deception, our nature is to still compare what we think someone else has (or is), to what we have, and who we are.

Advertising, the media, and the news reports don't help either. With the underpinnings of "lack" as the marketplace foundation that drives economic growth, we are unwittingly trained to think in " to enough" to compare, to demand more, and to blame others when we don't have what we think we should.

Bring this culture into relationships with individuals who are already struggling with their own life lessons, and now we have a hot mess.

Yes, relationships are more complex - and complicated than ever.

However…Called to Love is an antidote. Alisa DiLorenzo has beautifully redirected our focus on the highway of busyness to rest-stops that shift our thinking, our perceptions, and our default behaviors to the truth of what "is" and who we are.

Reading Called to Love was like "exhaling" for me. The words were carefully chosen, the lessons thoughtfully shared, and the stories prayerfully chosen for "such a time as this."

Thank you, Alisa for reminding us of the treasures within each of us - especially our spouses, whom we tend to forget are our precious gifts in our lives.

Manna Ko

Speaker and Author of Made for More

The second most important relationship experienced here on Earth is with the one you commit to on your wedding day! Alisa DiLorenzo has written an authentic and insightful book that uses the most incredible example this world has ever known (Jesus) to help you take practical and achievable steps towards a better marriage. Called to Love can be a launching point for a new and better life together.

Jeff Countryman
Lead Pastor Cape Christian

I've been a longtime Tony and Alisa's marriage ministry. They have a refreshingly unique way of encouraging married couples with the Bible's timeless truths and practical applications that anyone can achieve. Alisa's new book, Called to Love, is an instant classic that will be strengthening marriages for many years to come. Read this book and apply its lessons! Your marriage will be stronger as a result.

Dave Willis
Founder of StrongerMarriages.com and Bestselling author of The Seven Laws of Love

Called to Love is real life marriage wrapped in the promises of Christ. Alisa's ability to reach couples through her writing, coaching and speaking has been powered up with the Word of God. Anyone wanting to recharge their love for their spouse should take this 40 day journey.

Lori Mercer
Co-Founder of 24-7 Commitment

Having been married for 13 years with three beautiful children, and pastoring a church together, I wish we could tell you we always placed our marriage as a priority. Yet, during busy seasons and challenging times, we put other things before each other. Every relationship experiences ups and downs, but when you are down you need to do something about it! In order to get back to where you want to be as a married couple you need to invest into your relationship. In this incredible book by Alisa DiLorenzo she brings to life the words of Jesus in such a beautiful perspective for the marriage relationship. The truths presented can leave a lasting transformation. We highly recommend investing in your marriage by reading this powerful book. Blessings to you as you begin the journey to having the marriage you always dreamed of! And remember, no matter how good your relationship is, it can always get better!

Pastor Jon and Pastor Becky Heinrichs
C3 San Diego, CA

What could the words of a carpenter from 2,000 years ago mean to your marriage today? Everything. In Called to Love, Alisa DiLorenzo provides couples with powerful, practical advice straight from the Word of God. Do yourself and your spouse a favor and get this book.

Dustin Riechmann
Author of 15-Minute Marriage Makeover and founder of EngagedMarriage.com

CALLED to LOVE

Experiencing Your Best Marriage
Through the Words of Jesus

BY ALISA DILORENZO

ONE Extraordinary Marriage
14820 Deerwood Street
Poway, CA 92064
(858)876-5663

Ordering Information:

Quantity sales. Special discounts are available on quantity purchases by corporations, associations, and others. For details, contact authors at the address above.

Called to Love: Experiencing Your Best Marriage Through the Words of Jesus

All scripture, unless otherwise marked, are taken from The Holy Bible, New International Version (NIV), Biblegateway.com.

Italics in Scripture quotations reflect the author's emphasis.

CONTENTS

DEDICATION

To Jesus,

Thank you for loving me enough to call to me

so that I could in turn show your love to others.

To the ones that I am called to love…

Alex and Abby, thank you for loving me as only children can,

My parents, thank you for loving me as only a parent can,

Tony, thank you for loving me no matter what.

To You,

No matter what, you are not only called to love,

you have the capacity to love.

FOREWORD

A fulfilling marriage overflowing with love, joy, and romance. It is something everyone who gets married desires.

Each of us grows up with dreams of a life-long relationship that transcends the heights of even the greatest Hollywood love story. Yet many marriages get stuck in a "clash of wills" as you fight for your right to have your needs met and your "wants" declared supreme.

No one sets out to destroy their marriage, but sadly many relationships are fractured due to a lack of wisdom, effort and selflessness to make things the best that they can be.

The most fulfilling relationships are the ones where both you and your spouse are living with the express purpose of being a blessing to the one that God has gifted you with.

Philippians 2:3-4 says, "Do nothing out of selfish ambition or vain conceit. Rather, in humility value others above yourselves, not looking to your own interests but each of you to the interests of others."

Can you imagine if you approached your marriage this way? The divorce rates would be minimized, families would be healthier, and, all in all, the world would look a lot brighter than it does now.

"Called to Love" is a brilliant book that draws upon the wisdom, counsel and actions of the greatest servant of all time, Jesus Christ. Alisa has skillfully pulled together an engaging and practical resource so you can enjoy a marriage that experiences the kind of love and fulfillment you grew up believing for.

This book is the antidote for the selfishness that has plagued our relationships and will become a great source of hope, healing and wisdom for couples to glean from for many generations to come.

Ps. Leanne Matthesius

Lead Pastor, C3 San Diego

INTRODUCTION

A book like Called to Love doesn't just happen. In fact, if I am honest with you, it's a book I wasn't even sure that I could write.

Come with me to September of 2015. Sit with me in the auditorium of C3 Church in San Diego, CA. I know, San Diego is not a bad place to have to sit awhile. Look around you and see 800+ women spending three days together worshipping, learning and truly being in the presence of God at the Cherish Women's Conference. Sit with me and just be in God's presence.

It was here that this book began. It was in this place that I heard God speak to me. It was here that I realized that I was not following through on my call to love Tony. Yes, I loved my husband. Yes, we were intentional about our marriage. Yes, we had made a decision that divorce was off the table, repeatedly. Yes, we were in a good place. BUT as I sat there under the theme of the conference, Dream Again, I realized that to be able to dream again in marriage I needed to heed the call to love beyond what I was already doing.

As I spent three days with all of these women praying, crying, laughing and being spoiled by the conference, I heard God say, "You need to read the Gospels again. In the Gospels is my call to love. There is a message that needs to be told." What? Read the Gospels?

Now, I was raised in the Catholic church. I "know" the gospel stories. I've heard them countless times as I'm sure a lot of you have. Let's see there's:

Immaculate conception. Check.

Born in a manger. Check

Left in the temple. Check.

Water into wine. Check.

The parable of the sower. Check.

Walk on water. Check.

Hanging on a cross. Check.

Rise from the dead. Check.

In fact, I probably rolled my eyes at the idea of reading the Gospels again. "God, Why do I need to read the Gospels again? The stories have already been told by men and women much more educated than me on the words of Jesus. What could I possibly discover that hadn't already been shared? Who am I to think that I could share anything about Jesus?"

It's funny to share these words with you because even as I read them, I hear Moses say, "Who am I that I should go to Pharaoh and bring the Israelites out of Egypt?" (Exodus 3:11) or the words of Jeremiah, "I do not know how to speak; I am too young." (Jeremiah 1:6). Or even Gideon, "Pardon me, my lord," Gideon replied, "but how can I save Israel? My clan is the weakest in Manasseh, and I am the least in my family." (Judges 6:15).

Who am I?

I'm not qualified.

I am the least in my family.

God was telling me to open my Bible and read the words of Jesus because there was more that needed to be said. I didn't think that there was anything new in the words of Jesus. I didn't believe that he could use me to share the Gospels with others. Just like Moses, Jeremiah, and Gideon, I felt that I wasn't qualified and I used every excuse I had to tell God why I couldn't or shouldn't write this book. I didn't know what I didn't know and if I am truly honest with you I had become numb to the words of Jesus.

It's hard to admit that, but I know that I'm not alone. Sometimes you read something over and over again, and the words lose their significance. Sometimes you think that you know all there is to know so, "Why bother?" Sometimes, you have lost sight of who you are and what you are called to do.

The book that you hold in your hands is the result of being obedient to that call. It's the response that I had to reading the Gospels again with fresh eyes and a willingness to see what God had in store for me and you when Jesus came to Earth.

When God called me to read the Gospels again, it wasn't only to get me to spend more time in my Bible. Although, to be clear, that is NEVER a bad thing. God called me to read the Gospels because the words of Jesus contain the blueprint for marriage. Yes, the blueprint for marriage!

Reading the Gospels with the understanding that I was supposed to dream again about the mission that God had called me to changed everything. In every story, in every account and interaction that Jesus had I saw that these weren't just life lessons, these words were the manual that each of us needs to do marriage and be married the way that God intended.

I've often told coaching clients that when you get married, not a single one of you was lucky enough to be given the manual to your spouse, the cheat sheet to their desires and how to handle certain situations. What I didn't realize until that encounter with the Gospels is that while you may not have a specific manual for your spouse, you do have the only manual that you will ever need.

Jesus spelled it out. First and foremost you are called to love. You are called to love the one with whom you became one. You are called to love when things are hard. You are called to love when you feel impatient. You are called to love in the little actions and the big sacrifices. You are called to love beyond your wedding day. You are called to love when you would rather ignore the problems. You are called to love when all you can see is your spouse's faults. You are called to love when you are busy. You care called to love when you are hurt. You are called to love at all times.

You are called to love your spouse.

Everything comes down to this. That's what I had never read when I read the Gospels. I knew Jesus talked about relationships throughout the Gospels, but I had never stopped to apply them to my most significant relationship, my marriage. As you read through this book, know that Jesus is calling you to love your spouse. More than just calling you to this he is putting his hand out and showing you the way. It is my prayer that you will read these words and pray them over your marriage. More importantly, I pray that you heed the words of Jesus and respond to the call to love your spouse.

Love you guys!

Alisa

HOW TO BEGIN YOUR JOURNEY

Open each day with an expectant heart. This is your time to let the Holy Spirit invade your life and marriage. *Expect that you are going to have fresh insights* into your actions, your heart, and your marriage. Know that when you choose to read the words of Jesus, you will be transformed. *Journal your journey.* Create a record of your experiences. It's amazing what you will find when you choose to be observant.

Be willing to put down your thoughts and prayers.

Be willing to change.

Be willing to listen.

Be willing to look in the mirror.

Be willing to try.

Be willing to have an extraordinary marriage.

Be willing to love.

Because you have been called to love make a commitment to *journal your thoughts everyday.* When you do this you'll begin to see the transformation in your marriage.

SECTION I:

I THOUGHT I KNEW WHAT TO DO

Don't we all?

Each of us has, at some point in time in our marriage, convinced ourselves that we know all that we need to know. You know your spouse inside and out. You know how to do this thing called marriage.

At least you did, until that moment when you realize that your marriage isn't working, when you start to get a sense that the two of you are disconnected. One day you wake up and realize that you haven't had a real conversation or even a peck on the cheek in a LONG time, and you say to yourself, "What am I doing wrong? I don't know what to do."

You are not alone. In the process of realizing that you thought you knew what you were doing, you come to the humbling realization that you have no clue. That's when you need the words of the Gospels the most. That is when you need Jesus speaking directly to you and your marriage.

DAY 1:

More Than Just Words for Your Wedding Vows

*"Haven't you read," he replied, "that at the beginning the Creator
'made them male and female,' and said, 'For this reason a man
will leave his father and mother and be united to his wife, and the
two will become one flesh'? So they are no longer two, but one flesh.
Therefore what God has joined together, let no one separate."*

MATTHEW 19:4-6

From the beginning of Adam and Eve's creation, the idea that
man and woman, husband and wife, would leave their families and
become one has been woven throughout the Bible. It's not just a nice
thought. It's the way that we were designed to do marriage, in unity,
without separation.

Unity requires action. Two different people do not come by unity
easily. Each of you has different ideas, different ways of doing things
(this is why the toilet paper over/under debate continues to loom
large in marriage), different goals and desires. You are not the same as
your spouse. Thank God! The world needs both of you.

In learning to do life as one, as a team, you learn how to seek to
understand each other. You learn how to put other's needs into consideration with your own because it's not just about you. This person
that you said "I do" to is an individual with their own thoughts and
feelings and becoming united with them involves learning how the
two of you can and will do life together.

We've heard these words so many times that I think many have
become numb to what they truly mean.

"...and the two will become *one flesh.*"

The process of becoming unified in marriage is just that, a process. It doesn't immediately happen when the two of you exchange rings and have the big party. That's just the beginning of becoming. It happens in all the shared moments; it happens in the good times and the bad, it happens in the big moments and the small.

Becoming one happens when you choose vulnerability over self-ishness. It happens when you allow yourself to feel instead of just pushing your emotions away. It happens when the two of you realize that you can make it through the hard times because you are in the process of becoming. So often in marriage, couples look at the hard times, the difficult times and use those situations as an excuse to pull away, to do their own thing.

Marriage is NOT about pulling away to do your own thing or live in your own world. If it was, why even get married? Marriage is about pressing in, leaning into one another and God. He brought the two of you together; he will be with you in every moment.

"...let no one separate..."

You and I see it everywhere. This marriage ending because of infidelity. That marriage ending because someone isn't happy. This marriage in trouble because of addiction. Couples who are spending more time with their devices instead of each other. And the list goes on. Anything can become an opportunity or reason to separate.

That was not God's original plan for marriage.

The message that we get in the world is "any reason is a good reason to get divorced so go ahead and end your marriage." The Bible says, "Therefore what God has joined together, let no one separate." It is no wonder people are so confused. If any reason is a good reason to get out how do we stay strong and stand firm in the word that what God has joined together, let no one separate?

We have to be different.

We have to be willing to go against the norm.

We have to be prepared to say, "I'm going to work on this. I'm not giving up."

When you and I take a stand for our marriages, when we say that it's going to be different, when we say that we are taking divorce off the table, generations are changed. One couple living out God's word, serves as light to others. One couple choosing to not let anything separate them impacts everyone in their community and ultimately in the world.

When you commit to working through your challenges, it's a commitment to let no one or nothing come in between the two of you. It's a commitment to your vows. It's a commitment to the covenant that you made.

When others say:

It's over.

I'm not working on this anymore.

I'm not happy.

What they are saying is that marriage is a contract. These people are saying that marriage is performance based.

It's not!

What God has joined together let no one separate.

Contractual relationships can be severed. Covenant relationships cannot. Which one are you choosing and creating in your marriage?

My guess is that as you have read through this today, you have been thinking about all of the ways that the two of you have become one and are becoming one. You've also been thinking about those places in your marriage where something or someone is trying to separate you. It's time to stand up and declare that you are becoming ONE and that no one or nothing will separate you.

Jesus, I know that I have let many things come in between my spouse and me. You designed marriage to be a forever covenant, not an "as long as I am happy" contract. I declare that there is a shift happening in my mindset. I am choosing the covenant that I made with my spouse. I am breaking free of those things that have kept me from becoming fully one with my spouse. I no longer want to be half in/half out. I stand up and declare, Jesus, that I am ALL IN. I speak life into this relationship. I want to be ONE with my spouse in all areas. I want us to have a marriage that others look to as a model. I want others to see that our marriage is impenetrable. I want a marriage that can withstand the temptations of this world so that even if there may be reasons for us to separate, with you at the center, with you as the foundation, separation is NOT an option. Holy Spirit, make me aware of those times when I am crossing the line, when I am allowing something or someone to take the place of my spouse. I believe that in becoming ONE, Jesus, that there will be nothing that can separate us. Amen.

DAY 2:

Marriage Isn't a Fairy Tale

"I have told you these things, so that in me you may have peace. In this world you will have trouble. But take heart! I have overcome the world."

JOHN 16:33

I wonder how many of us stood up, on our wedding day, with the thought, "I wonder when our trouble will come? I wonder what storms we will face together? I wonder how hard this thing called marriage is going to be?"

My guess? Not too many of you. It's not exactly the promise of a "ride off into the sunset, happily ever after, Hollywood ending." I didn't stand in the gazebo across from Tony and think about the fights we would have. Or about the times that we wouldn't like each other, or about the challenges we would face (some of our own making, some simply because bad things happen).

I didn't think about the ways that he would disappoint or hurt me, and I know that I wasn't thinking about how I would hurt him. And yet Jesus said, in these three sentences, we do get the promise of happily ever after. It doesn't look like a Hollywood ending. It looks like a Heaven ending.

But take heart! I have overcome the world.

Put another way: Be encouraged. I've got this handled. Problems and challenges in marriage come. There's no getting around that in this broken world. That's when Jesus' promise that he has overcome the world is so needed. You and I, we don't need to believe in an overcomer when everything is going well, when we have just said "I do" and can't imagine any problems. We need that Savior when the job has been lost, when there has been a miscarriage, when it's been ages since there has been any semblance of a real conversation. That is the time when we need an overcomer.

Jesus tells us what's coming and he tells us that there is a solution. So often in marriage couples act like they didn't know what was coming.

"I thought that we had the fairytale."

"I believed that everything was OK."

"I didn't know that things could get this bad."

The truth is that not a single one of us was promised smooth sailing from the time that you said, "I do" until your final breath.

In those moments of struggle, trouble, and uncertainty, you each need to remember the power in this verse. Did you notice that Jesus didn't say, I have ONLY overcome the financial world? Or, I have ONLY overcome difficult family relationships? Or, I have overcome poor communication? No, he said, "I have overcome the world." All of it.

All of the bad, difficult, hurtful, disappointing, "I'm not happy," "I would rather quit" stuff, that's what Jesus overcame.

That's our model.

Jesus gets it. He told us that the challenges were coming so we wouldn't be surprised, so that in knowing that he had overcome the world we could not only have faith in our times of struggle but stand strong in his promise, "I have overcome the world."

No marriage is perfect, despite what you see on Facebook, Instagram or TV, and movies. Two imperfect human beings living together for more than a day are going to have their challenges. Some problems start during the wedding or the reception. The power in this verse is that we don't have to give up when faced with those challenges.

I have witnessed the miraculous in marriage. Think about the separated couples who restore their marriages. Couples whose finances were all over the place who are now "in the black." Couples who couldn't talk to each other without screaming and fighting who now have a real conversation where both sides feel heard and validated. Couples who were sexless now enjoying physical intimacy as a part of their marriage. In each of these situations, the couples had to overcome their challenges, overcome the blocks, overcome the hurt and they were able to because Jesus first overcame the difficulties of the world and set the example.

Did they do it on their own? Did they just put their head down and power through the tough seasons? Interestingly enough, and in contradiction to everything that the world wants you and me to believe, they did not. Each of the couples that have made it through and have seen restoration had a common thread, they had their faith. More importantly, they had a role model.

The world that we live in doesn't believe in overcoming, the motto is, "Give up and try again with a different person." When you choose to work through your challenges - together - you are choosing to be counter-cultural. Choosing to overcome the hurt, the pain and the disappointment, without bitterness, is such a foreign concept for most people.

We live in a world that says if you hurt me, I'm going to hurt you back, harder.

Overcoming isn't about forgetting the past. It isn't about pretending that it didn't happen. It's about gathering your resources and your strength to not only deal with the trouble but to emerge stronger.

Each one of you is an overcomer. Each one of you can create

something beautiful out of the pain in your marriage. You don't have to just tolerate the circumstances. Here's how I know. In our marriage, we have dealt with pornography addiction, financial stupidity (numerous times), the death of a child, questionable friendships, the short sale of our home, anger, lack of sex, living as roommates, living long distance, and the list goes on. In 2016, we celebrated our 20th wedding anniversary. An anniversary that, at times, I didn't think that we would ever celebrate. An anniversary that many don't even come close to reaching. Here we are, a couple who has and who continues to overcome life's challenges. How did we do it? We came to understand that there will be troubles but our God overcame the world for <u>us</u>.

Jesus, how many times have I thought that my life should be easy? How many times have I been frustrated at the challenges that I am facing? How many times have I tried to power through on my strength and with my own resources? More than I want to admit. Thank you for reminding me daily that YOU have overcome the world. Your acknowledgment that I will have trouble doesn't make it any easier when I'm in the midst of the storm but knowing that you have overcome the world, knowing that you have overcome death, gives me hope. As I stand in you, I have that same power. I have the ability to overcome the world. I have the ability to overcome the challenges that I am facing. Thank you for being my ever present help in times of trouble. I am not defined by my challenges. I declare freedom from the mindset that, "I am locked into my problems, and there is no way out." With you, Jesus, I can overcome! Amen.

DAY 3:

Are We Walking Together or on Different Sides of the Road?

In reply, Jesus said: "A man was going down from Jerusalem to Jericho, when he was attacked by robbers. They stripped him of his clothes, beat him and went away, leaving him half dead. A priest happened to be going down the same road, and when he saw the man, he passed by on the other side. So too, a Levite, when he came to the place and saw him, passed by on the other side. But a Samaritan, as he traveled, came where the man was; and when he saw him, he took pity on him. He went to him and bandaged his wounds, pouring on oil and wine. Then he put the man on his own donkey, brought him to an inn and took care of him. The next day he took out two denarii and gave them to the innkeeper. 'Look after him,' he said, 'and when I return, I will reimburse you for any extra expense you may have.'

"Which of these three do you think was a neighbor to the man who fell into the hands of robbers?"

The expert in the law replied, "The one who had mercy on him."

Jesus told him, "Go and do likewise."

LUKE 10:30-37

Mercy. Caring. Understanding. Even when it may not be warranted. These emotions can be such a challenge in our marriages. When your spouse has done something to hurt you, when there is pain in your marriage, which one of these characters are you most likely to imitate?

Are you like the priest who ignores the situation, pretending it isn't happening?

Are you the Levite, who goes out of his way to avoid the situation?

Or are you the Samaritan? The one who cares for and nurtures your spouse and your marriage in the midst of the storms?

We know that storms are a fact of life. There are times when we are hurt, in pain, disappointed and it can be a very lonely place. When your spouse is dealing with a situation like this they can feel alone, isolated, as if no one cares. This is the time when you can have such an incredible impact.

You can be the one to care when no one else will.

You can be the one to pour into your spouse when they are not able to do so on their own.

You can be the one to bring along the extra support.

How often do we choose not to get involved when our spouses are dealing with difficulties? Sometimes it's because we think we have to have all of the answers or the ability to fix the situation. We don't. Sometimes we avoid the situation because we feel helpless or we don't know what they need.

The truth is that if it's your spouse is facing a challenge it is impacting the two of you. It's not up to you or me to fix all of our spouse's problems. It's up to us to love them. Sometimes we forget that and choose to get all caught up in their drama when all we are supposed to do is show mercy and love.

Mercy… Five little letters that have the power to transform your marriage. Mercy is defined as:

compassion or forgiveness shown toward someone whom it is within one's power to punish or harm.

Choosing to care when you have the ability to hurt. You have that power in your marriage. You have the capacity to hurt your spouse and to care for them. Just like in this story that Jesus told. Each one of the passersby had the power to hurt the man who had been robbed. The priest and the Levite did so by ignoring him and walking on the other side. The Samaritan had that same power but chose not to exercise it.

He chose to cross to the same side of the road, to be with the man in his pain. And as they say, "It made all of the difference." In the case of this man in the Bible, the Samaritan's mercy was the difference between life and death. The man had been left to die, and two people walked right by him. Because of being abandoned, by the time the Samaritan saw him, he was in terrible shape.

How often is your spouse in that same position? More than you are probably aware. It's time to stop glossing over the problems. It's time to stop walking over to the other side. It's time to do what Jesus said for us to do. It's time to show them mercy. Why are you waiting? Your marriage's life is depending on you to act now.

I know it's hard. I know that there are times when you want to turn away. I know that there are times that you want to push them away. I know that sometimes rejection seems easier or even justified. When you choose to be like the priest or the Levite, you end up killing your spouse one rejection at a time. After a while, there won't be anything left of your spouse or the marriage. That's not what either of you wants, and that's not what God had in mind for your marriage.

God wants your marriage to be whole and healthy. God wants the two of you functioning to be able to fulfill your mission. It's impossible to do that when there is no mercy in your marriage.

Healthy couples choose mercy even when they don't want to. Healthy couples express mercy when the world is calling for vengeance or rejection. Mercy isn't always easy, but it is always worth it. Mercy is a lifesaver in your marriage. It is the example of Jesus in our world. It is love.

Jesus, so often I have found myself acting more like the priest or the Levite in my marriage. I have walked to the other side. I have ignored the pain of my spouse. I have been more focused on my needs than theirs. These are the times when I look back and see that my actions caused the tension between us to escalate. My actions did not make the situation better. Holy Spirit, I pray for my eyes to be opened to every opportunity to show mercy to my spouse. I no longer want to be the selfish spouse, focusing on rejection instead of creating an invitation, focusing on pushing them away instead of pulling them in close. Jesus, give me the strength when I feel weak. Give me the tools when I feel ill equipped. I want to be like you, Jesus. I want mercy to be my default setting instead of the one that I have to think about. I never realized how much power I had to cause pain or to punish my spouse. I break off that spirit of vengeance. Let me remember that my responsibility is to show compassion and forgiveness, just like you did. Jesus, make me more like you. Amen.

DAY 4:

But I Love My Family

'For this reason a man will leave his father and mother and be united to his wife, and the two will become one flesh.' So they are no longer two, but one flesh.

MARK 10: 7-8

There was one day when you and your spouse, stood before family and friends and professed that you were being united in marriage. You were a man and woman coming together to become one. Two different people, from two different families, choosing to create a new family, that would start with the two of you. On that day what you were and who you were shifted into what the two of you would become.

Sometimes the significance of that day gets overshadowed by the party, the colors, the decorations and the dress. It becomes more about the outside than the inside. More attention is given to what you are showing instead of what you are becoming. With the focus so much on the external show, a very significant part of this verse often gets overlooked…

For this reason, a man shall leave his father and mother and be joined to his wife.

Truth be told, it's both the man and the woman who are leaving their father and mother and being joined to each other. More and more, this separation isn't happening, and it is wreaking havoc on marriages.

From Genesis 2:24 we have been told that "a man shall leave his father and mother and be joined to his wife, and they shall become one flesh" and yet time and time again couples are allowing their parents to have influence in their marriage and they are suffocating under this weight. If you are old enough to get married, you are old enough to make your own decisions. Your marriage needs you to have separation from your parents. Your spouse needs you to have separation from your parents. It's critical for both of you.

Jesus knew that we needed separation, it's why he reminded us of the words in Genesis. He understood that for us to make our own lives with our spouses, we would have to cut the ties with our parents. You've probably noticed he didn't say "cut off all contact with your parents" or "ignore them completely for the rest of your life." He said leave.

When our kids leave the house, I cannot control them in the same way that I would if they were at home with Tony and me. I cannot control what they do or what they say. They have to make their own decisions. They have to deal with their own consequences. They learn to be independent. They learn what works for them and what doesn't. Every time that they leave the house is an opportunity for them to grow into their own person separate from the two of us.

That's what Jesus is talking about here.

Your parents have had the opportunity to grow, nurture and influence you as you have grown from a child into the adult who is now married. It is now time for both of you to recognize that that relationship needs to change. No longer are your parent's needs or wishes to be primary in your life. No longer do you turn to them first for answers to the challenges you are facing. No longer do you share the most intimate details of your relationship with them.

This is the place for your spouse. Is it easy? Not always. Is it necessary? Every. Single. Time.

When you choose to run to mommy and daddy instead of your spouse, you diminish the importance of your marriage. You make your spouse feel unvalued. That's not why you married them. You married them to build a life together. You cannot do that if your parents are still the primary voice in your life. You can't do that if your parent's opinion has a greater weight than your spouse's opinion.

Leaving your parents to become one with your spouse is a gift, a gift that begins with the engagement. This is a gift that you continue to give throughout your marriage. It's a gift that impacts more than just the two of you. It establishes the marriage covenant the way that God intended, with husband and wife at the center. It creates a framework for those in your community, especially your children.

Our society needs married couples who have become ONE with each other. We need married people who understand the bond between husband and wife. Yes, it's important to seek wise counsel from our elders, including parents, but not at the expense of the marriage relationship. When the two of you become ONE, you are unified, you don't have to doubt your standing in the relationship, you don't have to wonder who will be making the decisions in your marriage. Couples who have left their mother and father and become ONE stand out in a crowd, they stand out for their unity.

Jesus, I know that there have been times when I have failed to leave my mother and father and become one with my spouse. I realize the damage this has done, and I don't want this to be the pattern in my marriage. This relationship that you have given me is too precious. I am so thankful that you gave me parents that taught me the right, and wrong, things to do. I'm appreciative of the fact that, in their own way, they only want what is best for me. Jesus, equip me with the words to put guardrails around my marriage, to establish that the two of us are one, to show love and mercy while maintaining that our marriage is my primary relationship. Jesus, I want a marriage like the one that you have described, a marriage where we have left our parents and are one, as husband and wife. Amen

D A Y 5 :

I Want To Do What I Want To Do

"You have let go of the commands of God and are holding on to human traditions." And he continued, *"You have a fine way of setting aside the commands of God in order to observe your own traditions!*

MARK 7: 8-9

Guilty!

You and I are constantly bombarded with messages of how the world sees marriage. We see marriage as a reason to throw an incredibly elaborate party with little to no consideration for what happens to a couple after. We see marriage as a contract, as long as you are meeting my needs and doing what I want I will stay married to you. We see marriage as temporary. There might be someone better down the road, but you'll do fine for right now. We see marriage as unnecessary, why marry if we can have all of the benefits without any of the commitment?

Not a single one of these messages honors God or is in alignment with God's view on marriage and yet they are all acceptable in our world today. We have gone so far from the commands of God in order to be acceptable in the world. This mentality is killing our marriage foundation.

God did not give us temporary commands. The Bible doesn't say, "Love God when you feel like it or when it's convenient for you." He didn't say, "Love your neighbor when s/he's being nice or when s/he's doing things for you or giving you gifts." The Bible says, "Love the Lord your God with all of you heart, mind, soul and strength and love your neighbor as yourself." (Luke 10:27)

That's it. Everything that we are and everything that we do should come back to God's commands and NOT what the world is telling us. The world does not have your best interests at heart. We know that the enemy goes back and forth throughout the earth influencing man (see Job 2:2). This is the whole reason that our human traditions can become so corrupt. When you and I turn our back on God, when we turn away from Jesus, we allow our marriages to fall apart. We allow the influences of the world to color how we see our spouse and how we see our marriage. It's no longer about our covenant but rather all about my feelings.

We choose man-made traditions over God's commands because we like to feel good, we like our life to be easy, we like the quick win, we like having things our way. Yet how many marriages that have followed this path have been successful over the long haul?

Not many...if any.

Why?

Because this isn't how God designed marriage. He designed it to be according to his commands, not the way the world sees or values it. The Bible tells us that in marriage the two shall become one (Matthew 19:5), not two people leading two separate lives. Not two people intimately involved with others. The Bible doesn't give us the option to rewrite marriage. God told us to love others as ourselves, not to only love ourselves. God told us to serve, not to demand service. God speaks of covenants, not of contracts.

Marriage the way the world sees it is not working. We have more divorce, more broken families, more children splitting their time between two homes or more. You and I need to do marriage according to God's commands.

It's time to become one.

It's time to serve one another.

It's time to be in covenant with your spouse.

It's time to love one another.

We cannot wait for the world to figure this out so that we can start living the way that the world does. We need to be the example that the world follows. We need to stand up and say, "I choose to do marriage differently. I want to honor God's commands in my marriage. I want the covenant over convenience."

When we decide to do marriage like this people notice. There is a shift around you. You treat your spouse differently. You speak of them differently. You make different choices regarding your marriage.

It doesn't have to be this declaration, "I AM DOING MARRIAGE GOD'S WAY, WATCH ME!" That's just weird. Show it in your actions. Be the example that others look to because of your choices. Create a community where people can connect with you and see your marriage up close.

Marriage God's way is radical. It's life giving. It's empowering. It's possible. It's all about the choices that you make. Today choose God's commands over the world's ways and watch what happens to your relationship.

Jesus, so many times I have forgotten your commands, so many times I like what the world has to offer, at least on the surface. I want the quick fix. I want the easy answer. I have thought that the world's ways would bring happiness into my marriage. Thank you for never leaving me when I have gone down that path. Thank you for correcting me, for giving me guidance, for bringing people around me to speak life and discipline into me and my marriage. It is so easy to get caught up in the world, to see things from the world's view, that I lose sight of your perspective. I am grateful that your word on marriage is so simple, love and serve. Today, Jesus, I ask to see where I can love and serve my spouse. I've tried taking the easy, worldly way and it's only complicated my life. When I speak these words of love and serve, I realize that your way is the easy way. Love and serve. Your commands, spoken over my spouse and my marriage make all the difference. Amen.

DAY 6:

Whose Plan Are You Following?

"Father, if you are willing, take this cup from me; yet not my will, but yours be done."

LUKE 22:42

These are Jesus' words on the night that he would face the ultimate betrayal, moments before one of those closest to him would wound him deeply, on the night that his best friends wouldn't know what to do. It's a night that many of you have faced in your marriages. It's that tough decision that you never imagined. It's that diagnosis that you never imagined. Just like Jesus.

Jesus did not give up. Jesus did not change course. Even though the next few hours of his life would be excruciatingly painful, even though he didn't want to go down the path in front of him, Jesus didn't take matters into his own hands and change course.

How many times have you wanted to throw up your hands and just say, "I'm done. I'm not going to do this?" (I don't have enough fingers and toes to count that high.) We've all done it. We live in a world that says, "If your marriage gets too hard don't do it anymore. If your marriage requires too much from you, just skip it. Be comfortable. Take the easy way. Don't work too hard. Don't put too much of yourself in it. Just keep it as easy as you can." That's the world's view; it's not the example that you see in Jesus.

As Jesus prayed to God, the Father, on the Mount of Olives, he said these words, "Father, if you are willing, take this cup from me…" This is the point where most of us want to stop the sentence.

God, take this trial away from me.

God, make this easier.

God, why does this have to be so hard?

God, I don't want to do this anymore. I want my life to be easy again. I want to go back to the way things were. I don't want to have to endure the pain that is to come. Please just make this be a nightmare that I can wake up from.

I know I've said all of those phrases and probably a lot more when my marriage wasn't going the way that I had hoped; when Tony and I weren't living the married life that I had envisioned. It's human nature to want to stop when things get hard. We don't want to have to expend extra effort. We want the Hollywood fairytale, the happily ever after, the neatly wrapped up ending. And yet...you and I don't live in that world, we live in the real world. We live in the world that has to take into account both parts of what Jesus said. In the first part, Jesus' humanity is evident. Jesus speaks just like you and me.

God, make it all better. God, take this hardship away from me.

It's the second part of that sentence though that is the difference maker, "...yet not my will, but yours be done.[emphasis added]" Just as you get to a point where you don't want to deal with the hard stuff, Jesus did too. The difference was that Jesus then gave it to God. He told God that he accepted the outcome regardless of whether or not it was what he, Jesus, wanted.

More often than not I think we fight this attitude instead of embracing it. We believe that it should be our will that is the priority. We think that we know best for our lives and that because it's our life we should be able to execute our will over everything.

In my marriage, it has been God's will...

• That Tony and I learn to move through a season of pornography so that we can be a message of hope to other couples facing this same struggle;

- That we become a voice for others who have dealt with the loss of a child, so that we can bring hope and encouragement that marriage does not end when a child dies;

- That we share our journey of financial mistakes, debt and the loss of our home, so that others would learn that there is a way to overcome these challenges, together;

- That we learn how to recover from infidelity, rejection, and the "roommate syndrome," so that our children and our community could have an example of marriage restored;

- That we are transparent with the fact that our marriage has been less than perfect on so many occasions.

Please understand that in no way do I believe that God did these things to me. These circumstances were NOT punishments. They were not inflicted on me because I was bad or had done awful things. Each of these situations happened because we live in a fallen world, we live in a world where bad things happen to good people, we live in a world where our decisions have consequences.

It's not a question of "Why did God allow this to happen to me?" but rather, "How will this circumstance be used to bring glory to God?"

Just like Jesus, when bad things happen it hurts, it doesn't feel good, we don't want the pain to continue. Nowhere was Jesus jumping up and down and saying, "This is great, can I do this again and again?" The maturity comes in looking at these situations in our marriage and saying to God, "not my will but yours be done."

What does this mean in our marriages? What is God's will for your relationship? God designed marriage to be this amazing covenant between a man and a woman. God's will for each of his children is that they be healthy and whole. There is only one way to be able to answer the question of "What is God's will for my marriage?" is to spend time with God. It's reading your Bible. It's time spent in prayer. It's knowing

God, not just head knowledge but heart knowledge.

When you spend time with someone, when you talk to them, when you study them you start to learn what their reactions will be. There are times when you can hear their voice or imagine what they will say or do. Not because you have ESP but because you know them so well, you can predict what they might do.

Here's something that we need to change in our lives, our prayer life. Jesus didn't wait until things got bad to talk to his Father. It was something that he did all the time. Jesus spent time in prayer throughout his life. It wasn't just in times of crisis or desperation. It was ALL the time. He prayed for those around him. He prayed for healing. He prayed for comfort. He prayed for fun (remember the water into wine?) Don't wait until things are bad in your marriage to start reaching out to God and asking for a miracle. Can he do it? Yes! Does it always happen as fast as you want or in the way that you want? No. Remember, "not my will, but yours be done."

If you take the time to cultivate the relationship then when you find yourself in times of trouble you will still be able to say, "Not my will but yours be done." Jesus didn't want to face the horrible in his life any more than you want to face the horrible in your life. He didn't want to take up the cross. However, he realized that fulfilling God's mission with his life was more important. The same goes for you. The same is true for the seasons that you will face in your marriage.

Jesus, thank you for your humanity that you would ask to have the pain be taken from you. So often I have felt alone in my pain, alone with what I am facing. I have struggled with trying to control those things that are really beyond my control. Jesus, thank you for reminding me who is really in control. When you uttered the words, "Not my will but yours be done" I realized that I have been incredibly selfish, wanting everything my way. Break off the selfish inclinations of my heart. I need to remember that as much as I think I have the whole picture of what is going on in my marriage, I don't. It is only in relationship with you that I come to understand your will and more importantly your will in my marriage. It is so easy for me to get wrapped up in what I know, in what I think, that I lose sight of the plan that YOU have for my life. Let me become aware of the Holy Spirit working in my life so that I can respond. Equip me with the tools that I will need when things don't go as I would like them to go. Daily, I will remind myself that with you as my Lord and Savior there can only be one person in charge and that's not me, so ultimately it's not my will that can be done. Thank you for your influence in my marriage. I pray to keep my eyes focused on your will for my marriage. Amen.

DAY 7:

What Do You Want?

Then they came to Jericho. As Jesus and his disciples, together with a large crowd, were leaving the city, a blind man, Bartimaeus (which means "son of Timaeus"), was sitting by the roadside begging. When he heard that it was Jesus of Nazareth, he began to shout, "Jesus, Son of David, have mercy on me!"

Many rebuked him and told him to be quiet, but he shouted all the more, "Son of David, have mercy on me!"

Jesus stopped and said, "Call him."

So they called to the blind man, "Cheer up! On your feet! He's calling you." Throwing his cloak aside, he jumped to his feet and came to Jesus.

"What do you want me to do for you?" Jesus asked him.

The blind man said, "Rabbi, I want to see."

"Go," said Jesus, "your faith has healed you." Immediately he received his sight and followed Jesus along the road.

MARK 10:46-52

Blind Bartimaeus had been labeled by his challenges until he encountered Jesus. He had been known by what he lacked instead of what he had. It's something that happens to a lot of us. We get defined by our circumstances instead of being defined by who we are in Jesus. We get defined by the mistakes or the poor decisions that we have made instead of by what Jesus has done for us.

Here was this man defined by society for what he lacked. And what did Jesus do? He "saw" this man. He stood still and requested his presence. The man who could not see was seen by the Savior of the World. How many times have you felt like Blind Bartimaeus in your marriage?

You've felt unable to see what needs changing?

You've felt unable to see what needs fixing?

You've felt unseen by those around you, especially your spouse?

Bartimaeus had been sitting by the side of the road begging. Can you relate? I know that I have begged in my marriage. I have begged for understanding. I have begged for peace. I have begged for help. I have begged for the pain to go away. Just like Bartimaeus, begging for whatever I thought I've needed.

It's worth noting that when he found out that it was Jesus, his begging changed; it became charged with power. His begging became more urgent. "Son of David, have mercy on me!" Bartimaeus knew that something was different with Jesus. He knew that this wasn't an everyday encounter. He was aware that he had to do something and he did. He cried out to Jesus for mercy. He cried out for kindness in his desperate situation.

We've all had desperate situations in our marriages: infidelity, loss, financial disasters, family struggles. I know that I haven't always cried out for mercy, for kindness. Sometimes I just cry, often, I have blamed Tony and looked to him to fix it for me. It's what happens next that makes Bartimaeus' call to Jesus so impactful.

Jesus stood still and called for Bartimaeus. In the midst of a crowd of people, pushing and pulling, Jesus stopped for one person. It's not easy to get a crowd to stand still and yet, Jesus did. Then Jesus asked Bartimaeus one question: "What do you want me to do for you?"

What do you want me to do for you?

What is your most pressing need at this moment?

What do you want?

And Bartimaeus responds with the request to be able to see. He didn't say, "I don't know." He didn't make up some long story about the fact that he had lost his sight and this was such a tragedy and on and on and on. He didn't focus on the fact that this was somebody else's fault because they had caused him to become blind. Bartimaeus understood something that many of us need to learn.

First, if your spouse asks you a question they genuinely want to know an answer. Jesus wasn't asking him to be polite. He stopped, in a crowd of people, to ask this question. He wanted the answer. Second, I need to be specific with my answers. Bartimaeus wanted to receive his sight. He wanted to be able to encounter the world in a different way. This desire is what we are all looking for when it comes to change in our marriages or ourselves. We are looking for a different experience.

Jesus asked sincerely. Bartimaeus answered truthfully. Jesus gave freely. Bartimaeus received completely. These are steps in the formula for success in marriage: ask, answer, give, receive.

It's not rocket science.

Unfortunately, we often make it much more complicated than it needs to be. Jesus asks all of us the same question. What do you want Me to do for you? He's waiting for your answer and mine. He's waiting for the direct answer, not the talk in circles, not the "I'll just ask for something small." He's waiting for the whole answer. The answer that's scary and big and the deepest desire of our heart. Why? Because our relationship with God is in direct proportion to our trust in how big God is.

Jesus spoke over Bartimaeus, and he received his sight. Why? Bartimaeus believed that it would happen. He believed that this request was not too big for Jesus.

Have you asked Jesus for what you want in your marriage? More importantly, have you believed God for your miracle? It's one thing to ask if you have one foot out the door or are making a backup plan, just in case God doesn't work out. It's a whole other situation to trust in God to transform your life and marriage.

So often, we just want to bring the little things to God. We make our God small. We limit his ability to move in our lives because we think of him as a small god, a god who doesn't have any real power to create miracles. Instead, we need to be like Bartimaeus not just asking for but expecting to receive the BIG, the outrageous, the "it-can-only-be-God."

Jesus, I want to be like Blind Bartimaeus. I want to be the one that cries out to you when everyone else is telling me to be quiet. I want to know you so intimately, to know that you will not only meet my needs but that you will give me the desires of my heart. Jesus, I know that I have made you small. I have put my own limitations on you. I have said in my heart and through my mouth, that you cannot do X, Y or Z. I have allowed the lies of the world to replace the promises of your word. Today, I declare that I am free from this way of thinking, I know that I can ask anything of you. As a child of God, there is NOTHING that I cannot ask for. I am bold in my faith. I am bold in asking, I am bold in believing that you can bring healing and restoration to my marriage. I know that through you I can receive the sight that I need to create the marriage that I desire. Today I choose to answer your question of "What do you want?" Jesus, I want an extraordinary marriage! Amen.

SECTION 2:

MARRIAGE IS HARDER THAN I THOUGHT

Yes, it is.

Hollywood movies and New York Times best sellers have us all believing that the challenges that we face in our marriages should be wrapped up in 2 hours or about 300 pages. Our reality is often much different. It's not easy being married to someone who is as imperfect as you are. It's not easy to cooperate and share all of the time. It's not easy to make choices that put another's needs ahead of our own.

And yet...this is exactly what Jesus is calling us to do.

He calls us to have strength in the midst of the storms. He calls us to work on ourselves. He calls us to honor our vows. He calls us to be vulnerable. Ultimately, he calls us to love one another even when it is hard.

D A Y   8 :

Nobody Told Me Marriage Would Be This Hard

And being in anguish, he prayed more earnestly, and his sweat was like drops of blood falling to the ground.

LUKE 22:44

There are times in every marriage where it feels like you are pouring blood, sweat, and tears into the relationship, where it feels as if the very effort itself to make this relationship work is taking everything you've got. Jesus knows that pain. More importantly Jesus knows your pain.

Stop for a moment and think about the fact that Jesus knows what it is to be so emotionally invested in something that it comes down to blood, sweat, and tears. Jesus isn't removed from us. He isn't some god who has said, "You are on your own. I don't care about you and I'm not going to experience life the way that you live it." He hasn't left us to fend for ourselves. He poured out everything that he had for the most important relationship. The relationship with us.

Why would he do this? Because in doing so, Jesus provided us with a role model for what to do when the relationship was broken. Man had willingly chosen to break the relationship and yet, God, as Jesus, still chose to not just stay engaged, but to actively seek the repair of that relationship.

In choosing to restore the relationship, Jesus didn't just snap his fingers. He didn't just say, "All better!". He knew that true restoration requires effort. It requires time and energy. We all want the quick fix when our marriages go off track. Just make it better. Why do I have to do anything? I didn't mess this up, my spouse did.

Stop for a moment on that last statement.

Jesus doesn't mess up our lives, we do. It has always been man's sin that has separated us from God. Jesus didn't have to be the one to fix it. He could have waited for you or I, or any one of the other billions of people on earth to "figure it out." He could have said, "I didn't make this mess. I'm not responsible for fixing it."

But he didn't. He went into the garden and "prayed more earnestly." He prayed for you and he prayed for your spouse. He prayed for the mistakes that we have made. He prayed for the poor decisions we would make. Jesus prayed until it hurt. In agony, he went to God.

Jesus prayed when it wasn't his fault.

Jesus prayed for those who wouldn't acknowledge him.

Jesus prayed in a time of unbelievable stress.

Jesus prayed when he felt all alone.

The problems in your marriage aren't always the ones that you have created. You still need to pray. Your spouse isn't always going to acknowledge you or your efforts. You still need to pray. Your marriage could face stresses of many different kinds (affairs, broken finances, lost children, lack of connection, lack of sex, broken trust, lack of intimacy and many other issues). You still need to pray. There are going to be seasons in your marriage when you feel all alone. You need to pray.

I have to think that Jesus felt alone that night, wondering why and if all of this effort was worth it. One of the strongest tools of the enemy is the tool of isolation or loneliness. It is a lie that we are all alone, that we are the only ones experiencing, or who have EVER experienced, our unique circumstances. The truth is that while the situations may be different from person to person, the emotions and the feelings are as universal as the air that we breathe. We live in a world where people hurt other people, where there are times when it feels like no matter what we do things are going downhill and FAST.

Imagine Jesus as he prayed that night. As he prayed, he was in extreme anguish knowing what was to come. That's the same pain that you and I have felt in the middle of the night when the phone call comes, the anguish that we feel when we see the text message or walk in on something that we were never supposed to see, or the pain of the confession that we never expected to hear. You are not alone in your pain. You are not alone in your circumstances.

Our God, the God of the universe, has hurt just like you have hurt. He knows better than anyone what it feels like to have so much invested in the relationship and to want a different outcome. He knows what it's like to give everything and to still be hurting. Even with all of this he still pours into the relationship.

Let those words wash over you. Let them bring you comfort. Let them be a realization that while no human being may be able to relate to you at this moment that there is someone who can relate to you.

Jesus loves you so much that he chose to experience everything that you experience.

Yes, there are times when your marriage will require blood, sweat, and tears. As Jesus demonstrated to us, everything worthwhile will at some point in time need this investment of ourselves. When you find yourself in this place, remember that you are not alone. Remember that at any moment you have access to the One who can bring you comfort.

Jesus, how did you know that I would find myself in these seasons in my marriage when it would feel so hard; when it would feel like I am giving everything of myself and I still have to give more? It amazes me that you, as the God of the Universe, would willingly choose to feel the same pain that I do, would willingly endure the hurt. There are so many times when

I feel alone. Thank you for knowing my pain. Thank you for enduring this pain so that I would know that I am not alone. Jesus, be the rock that I cling to in this place! I often want to run away, to bury my head in the sand. Jesus, equip me to be like you. Strong enough to bear the pain, strong enough to move forward. Jesus, in my pain, let me find my strength in you and in knowing that I am not alone. Amen.

DAY 9:

The United State of Marriage

Jesus knew their thoughts and said to them, "Every kingdom divided against itself will be ruined, and every city or household divided against itself will not stand."

MATTHEW 12:25

In the times of Jesus, kingdoms were commonplace. The kingdom was the foundational structure for the people. It was their security. It was their framework for all aspects of life. It provided their relationships. It was their livelihood. It was their home.

If there was division in the kingdom, the kingdom was weakened. A kingdom divided was susceptible to attack. A kingdom divided would have to spend more energy on trying to come up with a working plan and more time trying to become unified. The lack of unity caused confusion. It created mistrust. It caused a lack of focus. It gave enemies opportunities to exploit weak spots. A kingdom divided was vulnerable.

The same applies to your marriage.

Jesus wants you to realize the power in unity and the danger in division. Your marriage was never designed to be a place of division. You were not created to do battle against your spouse. This is the reason that Jesus was so clear in his words about a house divided. A house divided will not stand. Neither will your marriage.

When I work with couples who are in crisis, I often ask them one of two questions:

What attracted you to your spouse? Or, Why did you get married?

Both of these are questions that focus on unity. They are questions that will take a couple back to a time when they were not divided;

when it seemed like they could and would do everything together. These questions bring forth smiles and knowing glances as a couple starts walking down memory lane.

Then there's a pause. The moment when things took a turn, when life got in the way, when the division started to come into the relationship. We live in a world where division is valued. It's a world of us vs. them. Good guys and bad guys. My way or your way.

We live in a world of division.

We live in a world that is destroying marriages. We need to be the antidote to this way of thinking. We need to be the ones to demonstrate that marriage is NOT about a house divided but rather a house united. It's not you vs. your spouse, fighting for your way, fighting to be right, fighting about everything. Instead, it's the two of you united against everything that would try to destroy your marriage.

If "a house divided will not stand" is true then the opposite is also true, a house united will stand. A house united against distractions will stand. A house united against addiction will stand. A house united against busyness will stand. A house united will stand.

Every day you have choice in your marriage and with your spouse. Will you be a house divided or will you be a house united?

I can tell you that in the seasons in our marriage when we have not been united we have struggled at every turn. We have seen each other as the enemy instead of looking at what we are dealing with as the problem. We have struggled with feelings of insecurity, jealousy, and selfishness. We attacked each other instead of our challenges. In doing so, we became vulnerable to outside influences. We opened our marriage up to attack from other people, individuals who have not always had our best interests at heart.

There are so many attacks on marriage these days, so many attacks on your marriage specifically, that you need to be united. You know what these attacks are. You see them and feel them on a regular basis. You know that when the two of you are united, spending time together, sharing your feelings, connecting on more than a surface level, you are equipped to fight off whatever comes your way. You also know that when you aren't spending time together, when you are not connected that it feels like the wheels are falling off of your marriage. You begin to wonder why this idea of marriage was a good thing. You wonder why you thought this person, your spouse, was the right person for you. These are all tools of the enemy to cause your house, your marriage, to become divided.

That's not the vision that God had for your marriage.

The two of you need to make a decision, no matter where you are in your marriage, that you are going to become a house united, a couple united. Does that happen overnight? No. Will there be days when you still wonder if it's even possible? Yes. Keep going! You need to keep working toward your goal.

Your marriage and your community need you. Our world needs more examples of unified marriages. We live in a world desperate for examples of marriage working, in spite of the attacks. The only way that will happen is if you CHOOSE unity, if you CHOOSE to work together, if you CHOOSE to find ways to cooperate. Together you are a mighty force, united for greatness.

Jesus, I have seen my marriage as a house divided. As I reflect on your words, I can see so clearly how the enemy has attempted to divide us in small ways, breaking off pieces of our foundation, opening up holes where we have become vulnerable. I can see that we have both done this. Jesus, strengthen us. I want us to be the couple that walks unified. I know that we do not have to agree on everything, but we have to walk this life together. Holy Spirit, open my eyes to the ways that I can be unified with my spouse. I want to be a stronghold for my spouse, use me to be the example in my marriage of what unity looks like. I break off those bonds that the enemy has used to divide us. Prompt me to find ways to create unity. We will be a kingdom united! Amen.

DAY 10:

I Feel All Alone

About three in the afternoon Jesus cried out in a loud voice, "Eli, Eli, lema sabachthani?" (which means "My God, my God, why have you forsaken me?")

MATTHEW 27:46

Jesus, fully God and fully human, felt abandoned by God. He felt like it was too much. He felt alone.

There have been countless times in my marriage, and I'm sure in yours too, when you felt like screaming out, "God, where are you? Why aren't you working here to make this better? Why haven't you fixed this? Why have you let us get this far into trouble?" Times when you have felt like God isn't listening, doesn't care and has completely stepped out of your life.

Isn't it incredible to think that the God of the universe, Jesus, as a human, felt the same way? Jesus who knew what was to come. Jesus who had a solid understanding of who He was, still felt as if God wasn't there in his darkest hour.

Tony and I experienced this when our son Andrew was born at 18 weeks. My water broke at 17 weeks and then stopped for a week until I went into labor on the night of our son's 2nd birthday. Even though there was no chance that Andrew was going to survive labor I was still placed in a room on the maternity floor. I spent most of December 14, 2004, having contractions and listening to other babies cry. I heard the joy of other families, knowing that that was not going to be my story, knowing that I would go home with empty arms. That knowledge didn't change the pain of what was to come or make it any easier. At 8:25 pm Andrew was born and a part of me died.

Just like Jesus on the cross I did feel forsaken. I felt all alone. I didn't understand why my arms were empty. I didn't understand that this grief was not just mine, but Tony's as well. This part of me died because I wouldn't allow love to work on my heart. I felt abandoned by God. Even though I knew better, there was a part of me that felt like I was being punished. It sounds a lot like Jesus' cry.

I was wracked with guilt, wondering what I could have done differently. According to the doctors, there was nothing I could have done but that didn't take away my mommy guilt. I hurt and in that pain, I pulled away from Tony. I pulled away in a season that could have brought us closer together. I pulled away because I didn't know how to lean in. I just knew that my arms were empty and my family didn't look the way that I had expected it too. In my mind, God had forsaken me.

In the midst of this storm, these words came to me. Words that Jesus uttered before I ever did. Even though he was in the fight for his life, Jesus did not stop talking with God. He did not withdraw from God. He did not run away from the situation. Jesus stayed on the cross and allowed the crucifixion to proceed. In that dark place, he uttered nine words that have the power to change your life and marriage.

My God, My God...

No matter what you are facing, no matter what the struggle is in your marriage, God is still sovereign, he is and always will be God. Personalizing this statement with "my" indicates the deeply personal relationship, the belonging. God is not just for other people. He is mine, and he is yours too. God doesn't ever check out of the relationship with us. It's us who pulls away.

Why have you...

It is OK to question our circumstances. It is OK to ask God why something is happening. Jesus did, and he knew the answers. So many times when you and I are facing things in our marriage we feel like we have to have it all figured out, like it's not ok to question, like we should just accept. It's OK to question as long as you are going to God to find the answers.

Can I remind you of one thing? God doesn't do anything to us. God is not out to get you or me. He's not in heaven thinking, "What can I do to make his/her life miserable today?" The problems that we face are because of human choices, because we have free will. God ultimately desires us that we have a peaceful, abundant life. When we turn towards God asking why he did, or didn't do, something it's often because it's easier to blame God, then it is to turn those emotions toward the person that has hurt us.

Forsaken me?

There it is, the expression of feelings. We have to develop the ability to express what we feel. Jesus felt completely alone and said that. It didn't change the course of events, but it did speak truth into the situation. Jesus wasn't afraid to say what he felt, and he wasn't just saying it so that those around him could hear it. He was saying it to God. I believe that this was a cry, full of emotion and pain. He chose to go to God in this place of deep distress.

Why do we so often run the other way? The pain that we feel when life doesn't go the way that we want, or when our marriages aren't going the way that we want is no less significant than what Jesus was facing and yet, the tendency is to bottle those feelings up inside. We live in fear of how people will react to our feelings instead of living in freedom from having our feelings expressed.

The abandonment that Jesus felt was not a permanent condition. It was NOT the end of the story. Restoration was coming. A better future was coming. Why? Because Jesus did not turn away from God. The same can be true for you no matter what you are facing in your marriage. There is always a better future in Jesus.

If Jesus can question God in the midst of the cross, you can too. If Jesus can express his feelings of abandonment, so can you. If Jesus can lean into God when it feels that all is lost, you can too.

God doesn't change. It is us who changes. It is our perspective that changes. While Jesus felt forsaken, the truth was that God had never been closer. God was in every moment of Jesus' pain, just like he is in every moment of your pain. Go ahead and express your hurt and know that God is there.

Jesus, you know that there have been so many times when I have felt abandoned and hurt. There have been countless instances when I should have cried out to you and instead, I've kept everything bottled inside of me. Jesus, there have been times when I didn't know if you saw me or even cared. Reading these words reminds me that you felt the same way. Jesus, this example is so powerful. I want to model my life on yours. I want to be able to express my emotions without fear. I pray for my eyes to be opened to know that in the midst of the worst seasons of my life, you are there. What an amazing relationship modeled in these nine words! God as Son, crying out to God as Father, in the midst of excruciating agony. Let me learn to cry out, not to be burdened but to experience freedom in my relationship with you. Amen.

DAY 11:

It's All Their Fault

"Why do you look at the speck of sawdust in your brother's eye and pay no attention to the plank in your own eye? How can you say to your brother, 'Brother, let me take the speck out of your eye,' when you yourself fail to see the plank in your own eye? You hypocrite, first take the plank out of your eye, and then you will see clearly to remove the speck from your brother's eye."

LUKE 6:41-42

The speck in your spouse's eye.

The faults that they have.

The mistakes that your spouse has made.

The hurts that they have caused.

The disappointments that they have created.

You should have done this.

I can't believe YOU did that.

How could YOU be so careless, inconsiderate, rude, heartless...

It is so easy to see what other's need to fix in their lives, especially if you are married to that person and know them "inside and out." You feel justified in your comments to your spouse often using the excuse, "Well, I love them, why wouldn't I want them to fix this aspect of who they are?"

Let's talk about their speck vs. your plank.

You know the difference but do you stop to think about it? Jesus is telling us that our problems, issues, mistakes are planks in our own eyes compared to the speck in our spouse's eyes. Why is that? It is because our own issues blind us from seeing clearly. When we don't deal with our unresolved "stuff" it colors every interaction with everyone that we come in contact with, especially our spouses.

If we are dealing with unresolved lies, we question everything that we are told.

If we are dealing with unresolved addiction, we are hypersensitive to other's behaviors.

If we are dealing with insecurity, we can find it difficult to trust others.

And the list goes on.

Often what you see in others is nothing compared to what you have to deal with in your own life. Not a single one of us is where we want to be. We are all a work in progress. The problem is that it's human nature to try and fix them without fixing ourselves first.

Jesus tells us not to be a hypocrite. He says that we need to "First remove the plank from [our] own eye and then you will see clearly to remove the speck that is in your brother's [or spouse's] eye."

You have a lot of stuff to deal with, and yet you often don't want to. Me too. It's easier to look outward. It's easier to put the responsibility for change on your spouse. It's easier to say, "If you would do this than we would be better" or "If you would only fix this then we wouldn't have any problems." I know from my experience and from what Jesus is saying here that both husbands and wives have things to work on, but it's not your responsibility to work on your spouse. Ever.

I probably don't need to ask this but I will. What happens when you start pointing out what your spouse needs to work on before you work on your own things? You know the arguments that ensue. You know how they turn it around and say something like, "What about you? Why don't you do this or that? Why is it always about me?" And the conversation goes downhill from there.

Jesus never told us to fix other people. He told us to care for them, he told us to be responsible for them but not to fix them. Our responsibility is to work on ourselves, create an environment for change and allow Jesus to work on them. Often we look at this in reverse: Jesus, fix my spouse and then I will be all better. It doesn't work that way.

Real transformation in marriage comes when we do just like Jesus said and first remove the plank from our own eye. When you work on getting healthy, when you work on healing the hurts of the past, when you choose to become the best version of yourself, you shift the atmosphere in your marriage. You create an environment where you can then speak lovingly to your spouse instead of in an accusatory tone.

When you choose, and yes, it is a choice, to remove the plank from your own eye first, you create an environment for Jesus to be seen in your marriage. Your spouse is more likely to see Jesus in the transformation in your life rather than when you try and change him or her. Most people are resistant to the change you try and force on them but not so resistant to a change in environment. Working on yourself first demonstrates humility, it shows surrender; it proves that you are a work in progress-not a finished work that is better than they are.

Marriage is about loving on one another, not condemning one another, not making one another feel bad or less than. When you are more focused on the specks in your spouse's eye than you are on your own planks you change that dynamic. You convey the message that they are not worthy, that your spouse somehow has to earn your love by doing or performing. That is NOT the message of the gospel.

Sometimes you and I become so blind to the planks in our own eyes that we don't realize how big they have become. When we do realize this, it seems like a monumental task to remove them. Do it anyway. Find those whom you can trust and ask them to help you see what you cannot. You cannot know where you are going if something is blocking your vision. Jesus wants you to follow him, to follow the path that he has you on. You need vision to get there.

Jesus, forgive me for all of the times that I have looked outward at what my spouse needs to change. It's easier on me to look at what they need to do instead of looking at what I need to do. Reading your word, I know that I have work to do. The planks in my own eye have kept me from seeing things clearly and from being able to fully love my spouse, as I see everything through my own pain. I know that is not the life that you intended for either one of us. Jesus, no more. I know that I am a work in progress. I declare freedom from those planks that are keeping me from a real, committed relationship with my spouse and with you. Holy Spirit, open my eyes to that which needs to be removed from my life. Equip me with the strength to walk out the life that you have for me so that I can better love my spouse and be the spouse that you have intended me to be. Amen.

DAY 12:

Jesus, If Only You Had Been Here

When Mary reached the place where Jesus was and saw him, she fell at his feet and said, "Lord, if you had been here, my brother would not have died." When Jesus saw her weeping, and the Jews who had come along with her also weeping, he was deeply moved in spirit and troubled.

JOHN 11:32-33

Oh, Mary! You speak for all of us in this moment. Stop for a moment and put yourself in this scene. Your brother was dying. The one person on earth that you KNOW could have done something took his time getting to you and in that span of time your brother died. "Jesus, why didn't you come sooner? Jesus, why didn't you do something?"

In this story, Mary is talking to Jesus about her brother but the truth is that you and I adopt this same attitude when things aren't going well in our marriages. Jesus, it's all your fault. Jesus, you should have changed the outcome. Jesus, if you had...

Mary knew Jesus. She had sat at his feet. She had listened to him and spent time with him and yet, in a moment of crisis, in her grief, she did what everyone does. She questioned his choices. We all do it. Mary just has her story of doubt recorded.

Every marriage has had experiences like this. Experiences where, through the decisions you made, the outcome wasn't what you expected. Marriages are full of times when the delay in getting what you want or in getting our "prize" has seemed like a denial from God instead of a temporary setback.

God's timing often doesn't look like ours or what we would want.

It's so easy to question God's wisdom through the filter of our humanity. We want lightning fast fixes to our problems. We want the answers that we want, right now. We don't have any desire to experience pain or heartbreak or disappointment. It doesn't feel good!

And yet, the real miracle would come later in this passage when Lazarus was raised from the dead. Jesus knew the outcome. He knew what each person involved was going to experience and he didn't change any aspect of this. The same is true in your marriage.

We each have our own journey. There are circumstances that we are going to be allowed to experience, no matter how painful. Jesus knows what you are going through in that season. He knows what you are feeling and it does matter to him.

Here's the piece that Mary didn't realize-Jesus was there. He was there when Lazarus was sick. He was there in Mary's times of worry. He was there when Lazarus was laid in the tomb. Jesus experienced all of it. The same way that he experiences everything that you are going through. Just because the answer isn't what you want, when you want it, doesn't mean that Jesus isn't there. It's up to us to seek him at all times, to know that he is there and that we are loved.

It's so important that this story is recorded in the Bible, because it let's us know that it's OK to question, it is OK to doubt. It is OK, as long as you take those questions and doubts to Jesus. There is no record of Mary complaining to her friends. You don't see her posting on Facebook, publicly shaming Jesus for what he didn't do. Mary was frustrated with her circumstances and felt Jesus was to blame. Instead of going elsewhere she went to Jesus. Mary went directly to the source.

You need to do the same.

When you are frustrated with what's going on in your marriage think about your actions. When you feel hopeless or lost please don't go posting stuff on social media. "It's complicated" on facebook does nothing to solve your problems. Don't complain about your spouse to your friends, most of the time you get sympathy instead of solutions. Instead do what Mary did. Go to Jesus. Tell him what you are feeling. Share your struggles. Be angry. Cry. Just like when Mary came to him, Jesus is able and willing to take all of your emotions. Go to Jesus, with everything.

Jesus, the blame game has been alive and well in my life. It's so easy for me to look and say things like Mary did. If only you had been here. If only you had done something. Jesus, as I read Mary's words, I realize that she lost sight of who you are just like I sometimes do. Jesus, open my heart to be more aware of your presence. I want to remember that I can come to you, no matter what I am feeling. I want to remember that you are always there, even when I can't see or feel you. Instead of complaining that you aren't doing anything, I seek to be aware of what you are doing. Instead of blaming my spouse, I want to have the heart to ask questions in a spirit of understanding and love. I don't want to keep everything locked up inside of me. I want to trust in you and in the journey that our marriage is on. Jesus, there are days, just like the day that Lazarus died, that I don't like what is happening. On those days and every other day, I seek to find your presence in my marriage. Amen.

DAY 13:

It's Time to Be a Light

"You are the light of the world. A town built on a hill cannot be hidden. Neither do people light a lamp and put it under a bowl. Instead they put it on its stand, and it gives light to everyone in the house. In the same way, let your light shine before others, that they may see your good deeds and glorify your Father in heaven."

MATTHEW 5:14-16

You are the light of the world.

This statement from Jesus is so incredibly empowering and yet most couples do not live as if they are the light of the world. In fact, most couples live as if they are sucking all the light from the world. You are empowered, by Jesus himself, to go and draw people to you. You have the choice to be an encourager and to bring light into dark places.

Look at the marriages around you. So many marriages today are characterized by negativity, discouragement, irritation and annoyance. I recently spoke with a couple who were dealing with this scenario in their relationship. The husband shared with me that he needs positivity and encouragement to thrive, and yet his marriage had become a place where this was not freely given.

There are a lot of reasons why the light may go out in you and in your marriage, but in these verses Jesus reminds us that we are the light of the world and that we are to let our light shine. Why? To bring glory to God.

Being a light in your life and in your marriage isn't about you. It's about God. It's about showing God's love and peace to your husband or wife. You have been given, by being married to him or her, the opportunity to point to God through your actions. People are naturally drawn to light. People are drawn to positivity. Are you drawing your spouse in or are you pushing them away?

There are so many little things that we allow to put out our light: irritations, annoyances, hurts, disappointments. Instead of dealing with them in the moment, instead of taking them to God, more and more people are trying to stuff them inside, trying to just power through. Little by little your light is going out. The problem is that when your light goes out, it doesn't just impact you. It impacts everyone around you. A black hole, a void, darkness, impacts everything around it. That's why Jesus told us that we need to... Let your light so shine before men

This light that Jesus is talking about is not dependent on other people's actions. It's not dependent on our feelings. The only thing that our light should be dependent on is our relationship with Jesus. When you are in right relationship with Jesus, you can't help but shine the light of God around you wherever you go. You know those people...the ones who light up a room when they walk in the door? The individuals who create smiles whenever their name is mentioned? Those are the people that are letting "their light so shine before men."

Their lives are not perfect and they have endured their fair share of hurts but that doesn't stop them from being Jesus to everyone, including their spouse.

You are the light of the world.

This is a mindset that each one of you needs to have, not just for yourself but for your marriage. When you embrace this idea that you are God's light in this world, there is a responsibility that comes with that and a motivation that propels you to do life differently.

When you chose to be the light of the world, in your marriage, it means that you:

- Make choices about your behavior. You can ask yourself is this behavior drawing my spouse to me (light) or pushing them away?

- Make choices about your words. You and I both know the power of words to either lift up and light up someone's world or to tear them down and plunge them into darkness. How are your words encouraging your spouse or are they a source of discouragement?

- Make choices about your attitude. Do you bring a spirit of positivity or negativity to your marriage and your spouse.

There are many poor messages about husbands and wives and society puts little value on marriage. When you embrace that you are the light of the world in your marriage, you have the privilege to transform the environment that the two of you live in.

Jesus did not say that we could be the light of the world. He wasn't talking theory. He said that you and I are the light of the world. This is our reality. It's time for you to start living this out in your marriage. It's never been more important. There are people everywhere desperate for more light, desperate for encouragement in their marriage. There must be marriages that give glory to God. It's necessary for every one of us. It's necessary for kids growing up who have never seen a healthy marriage. It's necessary for folks who have been hurt by previous partners and need hope that life can be different. It's necessary for you to know that your spouse has your back.

Jesus, because of you, I am the light of the world! These words are powerful in my life, and I know that all too often I choose to be darkness instead of light. I realize the responsibility that you have given me, and I walk into that today. No longer is it about me being comfortable in my darkness. The darkness does not point people to you. I understand what you are saying, and I know that it is my role, in the kingdom, to point people to you. It is my role to be a light in my marriage. I don't want my spouse to be in a place of darkness, and as the light of the world, I have the opportunity and the privilege to change that. I have never realized the power of this promise to impact my marriage. Today I walk in the light and choose to bring light to my marriage. I want my marriage to point to you. I want a marriage that can only be defined by what God has done for us and through us. Jesus, thank you for reminding me that I am the light of the world. Amen.

DAY 14:

All Things Are Possible

Jesus looked at them and said, "With man this is impossible, but not with God; all things are possible with God."

MARK 10:27

I can't do this anymore.

Marriage is too hard.

Why aren't we connecting?

I've tried everything.

I've said all of these phrases and more in our 20 years of marriage. There have been seasons when I have wondered if we would ever make it through. Seasons when we were dealing with debt, pornography, the death of our son, Andrew, and more. Seasons in which staying married seemed virtually impossible. You know those seasons, you have had them yourself, you might even be in one now.

Early in our marriage, I tried to power through the challenges that we faced. I read all of the books, spent hours on Google searching for "the answer." I tried to change Tony and then I tried to change myself. I tried saying "yes" to everything, and I tried saying "no" to everything. I tried manipulation and negotiation. I tried until I simply couldn't try anymore and felt like giving up. I tried until I realized that I didn't have the capabilities to create the change that I wanted. I tried until there was only one thing left for me to try.

Jesus

We live in a world that says "give up" or "move on" when things aren't going well in our marriage. We are encouraged to seek remedies for our unhappiness outside of our marriage, to end our marriages or to disconnect. We don't like life to be hard. We live in a society that has the motto, "Let's find the easy answer."

Isn't it ironic how the easiest answer of "Going to God" is often the last resort instead of the first strategy?

Life has been impossible for humans from the beginning. We are the product of a creator, not some happenstance. We have never been able to do the impossible on our own. God's hand has always been on the impossible.

Turn water into wine. God.

Raise a man who was dead for four days. God.

Make the sun stand still. God.

Feed 5000 with a few loaves of bread and a couple of fish. God.

Sometimes I think we just need to open our Bibles a little more to realize that we have no business getting involved in the impossible, especially when it comes to our marriages. Think about it...

Change his heart. God.

Make her more open. God.

Fix the finances. God.

Heal infertility. God.

Stop our fighting. God.

Mend our broken hearts. God.

Help us to move beyond the past. God.

We need to be involved in the process but we cannot do it on our own, nor were we ever supposed to do it on our own. We are wired to know when something is too hard for us or beyond our capacities. That's the feeling of overwhelm or the irritability that makes a mess out of us and our relationships. That's when we need to acknowledge that we are trying to do this all on our own. That's when we need to go to God and shout that we are at the end of what we can do. That end is the beginning of what God can do.

God is waiting for you to get out of the way of these situations in your life. That is not to say that you do not need to be involved in your miracles because that is simply not true. Time and again those men and women that received their miracles, many of whom we talk about in this book, had to take action for the impossible to become possible in their lives.

Not a single one of the miracles in the Bible happened without the presence of God in some way shape or form. Maybe it was Jesus performing the miracle. Maybe it was the Word of God spoken over the circumstances. Maybe it was those who had had access to God. In each case, God was involved. Why is it easier for us to look at the past and accept those miracles then it is to accept that God can still work miracles today? Why do we want to power through and show everyone that we can do it instead of relying on God?

We're like 2-year-olds saying "I DO IT. I DO IT!"

It is time to get over ourselves and allow God back into the equation. Jesus has told us that all things are possible with God. All things. Not just the easy things. Not just the little things. All things are possible with God.

It's time to stop putting our fingerprints all over everything. It's time to get involved in the miracle but not be the miracle worker. We don't have the capabilities to create miracles. What we do have is the ability to create an environment where God can work miracles. We have the capacity to create an atmosphere that is welcoming to God, an environment that says, "God, only you. Only you can do this thing that seems so impossible."

I've seen it happen in my marriage and the marriages of others. It was God who fixed our marriage after the death of our son. How do I know? Because I had completely shut down from Tony and life. I was like the walking dead, functioning but not present. Tony was trying to reach me, but we were both so broken. It was God who paved the way for us to find our way back to one another.

It was God who restored a client's marriage where she had left with half the money and half the furniture not knowing if they could survive the damage in their relationship. It was God who has restored couples after broken trust, after infertility, after wayward kids. None of these happens in your strength. It is only possible with God.

Jesus, thank you for the reminder that ALL things are possible with YOU. Thank you that there are no exclusions to this. Thank you that it's not just the little things or the easy things but that all things are possible. I know that I have, many times, tried to power through and do things completely on my own only to be frustrated and exhausted by the process. Thank you that you never give up on me. Thank you for letting me be a part of the process. Holy Spirit, open my eyes when I start to feel overwhelmed and irritated. Let this be a sign to me that I am trying to do the impossible on my own. A sign that I am trying to squeeze you out of the equation. Jesus, I know that I am not equipped to create all of the miracles that I want in my life. I pray for a willing heart and a spirit to work with you and not independent of you. Amen.

S E C T I O N   3 :

GET ME OFF OF THIS ROLLER COASTER

Sometimes marriage feels like it is two steps forward, three steps back. You're happy one minute and sad the next. You're going along on a seemingly straight path only to find yourself in a corkscrew, upside down and backward.

It's easy to feel like you are hanging on for dear life, to feel out of control and all alone. We live in a world that is seemingly connected and yet because of technology we feel less connected than at any other time in history.

Jesus doesn't want you to be on that roller coaster. He wants you to know that you are not in this life by yourself. He is with you every step of the way, no matter what you are facing. Even when it is hard to love your spouse, Jesus is there. He is there loving you, and he is there loving your spouse. He offers you his peace, the peace that transcends all understanding.

Do Not Be Afraid

Then Jesus said to them, "Do not be afraid."

MATTHEW 28: 10

Four powerful words that say everything there is to know about the human condition.

Do not be afraid of what has happened.

Do not be afraid of what is happening.

Do not be afraid of what will happen.

Jesus simply said, "Do not be afraid." It's a message that you are to take to heart and live out every day. We live in a world that embraces fear and your marriage is being impacted by your fears.

Fear of...

- Rejection

- Financial loss

- Wayward children

- Infidelity

- Drifting apart

- Not talking

- Addiction

- Not having sex

- Not having anything in common

- Only being focused on the kids

- Losing yourself and the list goes on.

Jesus did not say, "Do not be afraid, except for_____. He said, "Do not be afraid."

In Jesus we don't have to worry. In Jesus we have strength. In Jesus we have security. Fear comes from not knowing where your foundation is or who you are depending on. Fear comes when we lose sight of our anchor. Fear wreaks havoc on marriages. Fear makes us feel less than. Fear is destructive.

This is why Jesus tells you not to be afraid. He doesn't want you to be consumed with negative thoughts. He doesn't want you to live looking over your shoulder instead of looking ahead. When you are constantly looking in the past you are missing out on what's happening right now. When you are fixated on what has happened and what might happen you miss out on what IS happening.

Why are you so scared to live? Why are you so scared to be involved in your marriage?

I know that you have been hurt in the past. I know that you have been disappointed. More importantly, Jesus knows. He knows better than anyone what you have had to deal with and he still tells you, "Do not be afraid." He knows what's coming in your life and he tells you, "Do not be afraid."

It's been incredible to witness coaching clients break free of their fears, to realize that what they were afraid of has kept them from taking the action that they need to. One husband was so afraid of what to say or how to approach his wife that over time they just stopped talking to one another, drifting apart until they seemed like strangers. As he worked through his fears, he realized that he had been afraid of what his wife's reactions might be. By not acting on that fear and working through it he created an environment where they lost connection and instead of having to fear her reaction he found himself in a place where there was no interaction. He knows now that pushing through that fear would have allowed them to have connection instead of losing touch with one another.

A wife that I worked with, feared speaking up for herself. She worried that her husband wouldn't value her opinion and so she trained herself not to say anything, allowing that fear to grow and take over her life. The fear told her that he didn't care. The fear made her feel less than. It wasn't until she was able to find her voice and speak up that their marriage started to change for the better. She now has a voice in the marriage, it's the voice that her husband fell in love with. The voice that he's missed for so long. Her fear of what might happen almost cost her her marriage.

That's the thing about fear, it has a very high price. Feeding into fear costs you a lot of energy both mentally and physically. You become consumed with thinking through a thousand what if scenarios, you rehearse every possible conversation, changing your words or your spouse's words to make everything come out OK. You spend hours trying to create perfect scenarios. You spend so much time doing everything instead of engaging in the relationship.

Jesus told all of us, "Do not be afraid." It wasn't a suggestion. It wasn't something to make you feel better. It was a command. Do not live your life in a place of fear. Do not approach your marriage from the filter of fear. Do not let fear cripple you. Do not let fear keep you from having the marriage, from having the life that you were meant for.

What will it take for you to stop believing the lies of fear? What will it take to step out in courage, in confidence? Jesus is waiting for you. He's waiting to empower you to face your fears. You have the comfort of the Holy Spirit so that you don't have to do this by yourself.

For most people that's the biggest fear. That you are in this by yourself and you have to fix everything on your own. That's a lie. You have access to the power of the Holy Spirit. The same spirit that cast out demons and caused the storm to calm is in you. That power is waiting for you to tap into it. That power doesn't co-exist with fear, that power casts out fear.

Call on the name of Jesus when you are feeling fearful in your marriage. Ask Jesus for his strength when you are feeling like you can't do it on your own. You are not by yourself. You don't have to rely on what you can do or what you know.

You have Jesus.

You need nothing else.

It all starts there.

Do not be afraid to have the hard conversations.

Do not be afraid to try something new.

Do not be afraid to start over again with your spouse.

Do not be afraid to forgive.

Do not be afraid to look forward.

Do not be afraid to extend grace.

Knowing that you have Jesus is the strength that you need. Look to him. Embrace his words. Allow him to speak into your life. Look for opportunities to see Jesus and to be Jesus in your marriage. There are three of you in your marriage and together you make an unbeatable team.

Jesus, thank you for your power. Thank you for your strength. Too many times I have been afraid to step out. Too many times I have been afraid to say anything. I don't want fear to be a factor in my marriage. Today I declare freedom from fear. Today I declare that with you and in you, restoration is possible, our marriage is possible. Jesus, I have allowed fear to dictate the words that I say and the actions that I have taken. I have allowed the lies of the enemy to keep me from doing what I knew to be right, to keep me from loving my spouse in the way that they needed to be loved. No more, Jesus. I know that I am not doing my marriage by my-

self. I know that you are with me. I know that your perfect love is what I need to cast out my fear. I know that you are the answer to my fears. I understand that for my marriage to be all that you intended it cannot grow on a platform of fear, rather it grows in love. Today, Jesus, is the day that I turn my fears over to you. I choose to not let fear have power in my marriage. Amen

DAY 16:

I Just Want to Cry

Jesus wept.

JOHN 11:35

Jesus, the God of the universe, showed deep emotion.

Jesus knew how the story would end and he still wept. Jesus wept at the loss of his friend. Jesus wept in pain. In this particular story, Jesus is crying at the death of Lazarus, his friend. His weeping causes those around him to say, "See how much he loved him." John 11:36

Here was a man openly sharing his feelings in front of men and women. And yet, more and more I hear about couples that never share their emotions. They are so afraid that they just stuff their feelings until they are miserable.

Why have you stopped showing emotion in your marriage? Why do you have to hold it all inside of you? What made you believe that showing emotion is a sign of weakness, a sign that you can't handle life?

As a man, Jesus wept when he found himself in distressing circumstances. Why do you think that you are better than God, why do you think that holding in your emotions makes you superior to your spouse?

Newsflash: Holding in your emotions just makes you emotionally constipated.

Ignoring your emotions never fixes the problem it only delays dealing with them. When you stuff the hurt and pain, the negativity and disappointment inside of you, it causes you to treat people harshly. These actions create walls in your relationships. These emotions cause you to distance yourself from others so that you don't have to feel.

You cannot shut off your feelings forever. You cannot stuff these emotions into yourself without something breaking. That something could be yourself, it could be your marriage, it could be your job, it could be relationships with others. Your emotions are important. They are so important that Jesus not only expresses them, he shares them in front of other people.

"Jesus wept" is the shortest verse in the Bible and one of the most powerful. The Gospel writer, John, chose his words carefully in order for each of us to understand how important this concept is. The description of Jesus in this verse does not get hidden under a bunch of words. There aren't names that are difficult to understand. There's no need to get out the history books to understand the context here. It is simply two words, nine letters of significance.

Jesus, fully God and fully human, shows the same emotion that you and I have when we are hurt, when something has an overwhelming impact on us. John does not say that Jesus looked around to make sure that no one was watching. He doesn't say that Jesus went off by himself to have a good cry. He doesn't say that Jesus shed a single (movie-style) tear. John says that Jesus wept.

Dictionary.com defines weeping as expressing grief, sorrow, or any overpowering emotion by shedding tears. The two components of this definition are powerful: the expression of an overpowering emotion by the shedding of tears. I sometimes think that we humans don't see God as capable of overwhelming emotions. I know that there are times when I think of God as just this mellow kind of guy, not super happy, not super low-just going with the flow. My perspective is not biblical when I am thinking that. Jesus didn't just feel deeply then; he continues to feel our human condition now. Your God knows your pain. He cries along with you in sorrow and grief.

Why are you stuffing your emotions inside of you?

My guess is, it's because you think it's easier. Because you think that your spouse doesn't care. Because you don't think that your feelings are significant. Because if you open the door to expressing one emotion, you might find a whole bunch of other ones that you can't handle.

LIES. All of it lies. Lies that are keeping you from the life that God has created just for you.

I will share with you that I used to be that person. I used to be the one who wouldn't say anything, who found it easier to stuff my feelings than deal with them, who didn't want to rock the boat. And I was miserable. When I lived like this, I would stuff and stuff and stuff until there wasn't any more room and then I would explode. Not a good combination for marriage.

Your spouse and your marriage need intimacy on all levels including emotional intimacy. The two of you need to be able to share your feelings in a way that is safe and healthy. Why? Because Jesus did.

Look at little children, when they are loved and nurtured they know that if they have any pain that they can cry out, and someone will come and take care of them. For so many of us, we stopped having those needs met by other people because we received messages like:

- Stop crying.

- There's nothing to cry about.

- You cry all the time.

- Stop being a crybaby.

- Boys don't cry.

- Grow up.

These hurtful words taught you that expressing your grief or sorrow wasn't ok. And yet, the Bible tells us that Jesus wept. No one called the Son of Man a crybaby. No one told him that boys or men don't cry.

Jesus expressed a very real emotion, one that you and I both have and one that needs to be expressed when we are feeling it for the health of ourselves and our marriages. You don't need to be immobilized by these messages from your past. You can have a marriage in which vulnerability is not only accepted but is valued. It's time to take off the masks that the two of you have been living behind and to start living as Jesus lived, including the emotions that you have.

Jesus, thank you for being a man that was not afraid to show emotions. Thank you for showing us that our ability to express these emotions does not make us less than or inferior to others, rather our emotions allow us to connect with others. Jesus, I pray for my marriage to be a safe place to express my emotions. I declare that in recognizing my emotions and expressing them in a healthy way that I will strengthen my marriage. No longer will I believe the lie that expressing my emotions is a sign of weakness. No longer will I believe the lie that my feelings don't matter. Jesus, it's not just about me, though, let me be a safe place for my spouse to express his or her feelings. Equip me with the capability to comfort them, to be a listening ear or a comforting arm. In you and your example, I see the strength in expressing emotions. I see the freedom in being real. Jesus, that is what I want for my marriage. Amen.

DAY 17:

Why Are You Doing Things This Way?

While Jesus was in Bethany in the home of Simon the Leper, a woman came to him with an alabaster jar of very expensive perfume, which she poured on his head as he was reclining at the table.

When the disciples saw this, they were indignant. "Why this waste?" they asked. "This perfume could have been sold at a high price and the money given to the poor."

Aware of this, Jesus said to them, "Why are you bothering this woman? She has done a beautiful thing to me. The poor you will always have with you, but you will not always have me. When she poured this perfume on my body, she did it to prepare me for burial. Truly I tell you, wherever this gospel is preached throughout the world, what she has done will also be told, in memory of her."

MATTHEW 26:6-13

I can feel the frustration coming from the disciples. Why are you doing things this way? Why isn't that money being spent on something else? What's going on here? Frustration, confusion, and irritation all wrapped up in "Why this waste?" they asked. "This perfume could have been sold at a high price and the money given to the poor."

And then there is Jesus' response, "Why are you bothering this woman? She has done a beautiful thing to me."

Marriage is full of these type of moments.

Why did you spend money on that?

Why did you tell the kids they could go there?

Why are you texting that person?

Why are you staying up so late?

It seems that in many marriages, there comes the point where the couple isn't having conversations but rather just flinging accusatory questions at each other. Accusations are an interesting tool that we use to wound one another. In our questioning, we are breaking down the communication with our spouses instead of checking ourselves and our motivation before ever opening our mouths.

The disciples were irritated at the perceived extravagant waste of this woman. They felt that she could have made better choices. They felt that the money should have been spent differently. They felt that more people could have been impacted. BUT instead of approaching this situation with love, they spoke to her, and to Jesus, with irritation.

This has been my approach more times than I want to admit. When I see something happening in my marriage, I am quick to make a snap judgment instead of asking thoughtful questions to understand. The disciples did not desire an understanding of her motivations. They wanted their needs met. They wanted what they wanted, the oil sold and given to the poor. They couldn't see the bigger picture. They didn't understand that there were more factors involved and at the moment they didn't care.

How many times have you conveyed to your spouse that you don't care about them in the words that you have chosen?

It's interesting that the disciples asked, "Why this waste?" They could have asked this question from a place of love and concern, and yet they chose words of negativity. You can hear their tone of voice in the words chosen. You can hear the dismissiveness in their words. Her actions were not important. What she was doing was insignificant in their eyes. In their opinion, her choices were uninformed, ridiculous and just didn't make sense. It's painful to admit that I have shown this same negativity toward Tony.

When I look at the disciples, I don't see men who set out to be hurtful, and I honestly believe that most spouses aren't intentionally mean to one another. The disciples were people, just like you and me, who were learning how to be in a relationship with one another and who didn't always get it right.

And then there is the careful correction from Jesus, "Why are you bothering this woman? She has done a beautiful thing to me. The poor you will always have with you, but you will not always have me. When she poured this perfume on my body, she did it to prepare me for burial. Truly I tell you, wherever this gospel is preached throughout the world, what she has done will also be told, in memory of her."

Jesus stops the flow of negativity and provides an explanation for her actions. Jesus didn't get defensive. He didn't tell the disciples that their questions were irrelevant or stupid. Jesus didn't evade the situation. He simply shares the "why" to help the disciples understand.

More often than not when we get questioned by our spouse, our reaction is, "Why are you asking me that? Why do you want to know? Why do you ask me so many questions?" Our lack of transparency will always be met with more questions, more irritation, more frustration. Jesus provides the answer to minimizing frustration and anger in our conversations. Provide the answer and give an explanation.

Now, we may not always like the answer that we receive. That's something that is a part of marriage. However, when an explanation is delivered in a spirit of love, with the purpose of understanding, the entire dynamic in the marriage changes. It's that spirit of love that diffuses the situation. It's why we don't read of the disciples getting angrier or shouting at the woman. There was no need after they had received the explanation from Jesus. The same is true in our marriages.

We are all going to experience situations with our spouse where the irritation levels are very, very high. The decisions that we make in that place will determine so much for the future of our marriage. Will you hold onto your irritation and frustration and continue in that tone of voice OR will you be like Jesus and stop to understand the circumstances, to know what the motivations are? It's a choice that each of us needs to make, every single time.

Jesus, equip me with your perspective. So many times I have held onto that accusatory tone. I have been in that place where I am not seeking to understand my spouse, and I am only trying to make them feel bad or feel less than. That is not what you want of me or our marriage. I seek to be sensitive to the promptings of the Holy Spirit, to be aware of those times when I need to change not only my tone of voice but the words that I am choosing in speaking to my spouse. Jesus, I want to understand my spouse. I want to be a safe place for them to be able to share their choices and their motivations. I want us to have conversations based on connection and not condemnation. Jesus, thank you for showing me how understanding diffuses irritation. Let me take this knowledge into every encounter with them. I know that the only way that this will happen is to seek you in every situation. The disciples had you in their presence, and I have you in my heart. Let my words and my heart reflect you in how I treat my spouse. Amen.

DAY 18:

I'm Drowning Here!

As they sailed, he fell asleep. A squall came down on the lake, so that the boat was being swamped, and they were in great danger.

The disciples went and woke him, saying, "Master, Master, we're going to drown!"

He got up and rebuked the wind and the raging waters; the storm subsided, and all was calm. "Where is your faith?" he asked his disciples.

In fear and amazement, they asked one another, "Who is this? He commands even the winds and the water, and they obey him."

LUKE 8: 23-25

I am overwhelmed.

I'm drowning here.

I don't think we are going to make it.

Why isn't God here?

Why isn't God doing something?

I've thought this. I've felt it deep within my bones, within my soul. I've wondered where God was when our marriage was in trouble. I've thought that God stepped out of my life or had fallen asleep on the job. If you are truthful with yourself, you've had those same thoughts at different seasons in your marriage as well.

A windstorm came down on the lake...

God did not make the storm to punish them. He did not send the storm to "teach them a lesson." The storm came. Just like storms have come into your marriage. Storms that you didn't expect, in areas that you thought were secure. Here is a group made up of fishermen; these people knew the water. They knew what to expect and yet this storm caught them off guard. Storms do that. It's something that we all experience. You are not the only one going through a storm, and you are not alone in your storm.

They were filling with water…

What are you filling with in this season? Fear, anger, depression, resentment? I don't know what this storm is causing in you, what I do know is that as the negative thoughts start to accumulate, you feel like you are drowning. You feel like the world is against you. The what-ifs are consuming you. What could I have done? The truth is that there are times when there is nothing you could have done to prevent the situation.

They awoke him…

I love this image of Jesus sleeping while there is so much going on around him. It's an interesting perspective in contrast to how we feel when things are out of control. We feel like everyone should be frantic just like we are. And Jesus, he's sleeping. Why isn't he bothered by the rocking of the boat? Why isn't he crying? Why isn't he afraid? It is because Jesus knows the outcome and Jesus knows the power at his command. The power that you and I have as well. I often wonder, as I read this passage, what our lives would look like if we were able to be calm and relaxed instead of reacting during every storm.

saying, Master, Master we are perishing…

It's interesting to think about our perspective in light of what is truly going on. These fishermen thought their lives were over. The could see no hope in the situation, but that wasn't the truth. They brought more drama in the words that they spoke to themselves. They weren't looking for a solution they only wanted to talk about the problem. I've been there and done that. You probably have too. It's the whole "sky is falling" mentality. Let's just talk about the problem instead of looking for a way to resolve it. Talking can be helpful BUT only if it leads you to take action. Talking for the sake of rehashing the situation does NOTHING.

He rebuked the wind and the water...

Doesn't that sound overly easy? Just tell the storm to go away and leave you alone. Don't you just wish you could do that? Here's a little insight-You CAN. Maybe it won't look like immediate calm in the world around you, BUT there will be calm in your spirit. When you call on the Holy Spirit to be with you, when you take authority and speak the name of Jesus over that which threatens to destroy you, life changes. You change.

When my water broke at 17 weeks with our second child, I was immediately thrust into the world of specialists with all of their advice, all of their suggestions, all of their fear. It was a whirlwind of doctor's visits and opinions. Everyone had something to say about what was going on with our baby and with me. I remember crying and saying God, Why me? Why this baby? Why would you allow this to happen? Why is this baby going to perish? What have I done? Here I was expressing the same doubts that the 12 had and getting the same answer.

Where is your faith?

Where was my faith? Like so many, I had become consumed with the fears and the dire opinions that were being voiced around me. I could not see, at the time, how God could ever work any of this situation for good. I didn't understand at the time that this was part of my journey and not a punishment. I was afraid, yet, I had to believe.

My faith came in the quiet moments when I could just be with the situation and not let it consume me. It was in the quiet when I could hear God say, "I've got this. It will be OK." It was in the nurses who loved me and bore my grief as their own. Nurses who, I am convinced, were angels sent to be God's presence in that dark place. It was in Tony's presence by my side through all of the appointments and during that long night in the hospital when he never left my side.

I don't know what storm you are facing or what your marriage has faced. What I do know is that, in the midst of the storm, you can have peace. I do know that God is writing this storm into your testimony.

And they were afraid, and marveled, saying to one another, "Who can this be? For He commands even the winds and water, and they obey Him!"

The storm hadn't ended yet, and these 12 were marveling at the impact of the presence of Jesus in that place. They could see the beginning of the calm because Jesus had rebuked the wind and the water. Jesus was invited into the storm, and those in the storm experienced a shift. They could see the power of Jesus and while they didn't understand they knew it was having an impact on each one of them.

Jesus IS your life preserver. He is the one who calms the storms and brings a sense of peace. The power in Jesus is available to you and your marriage. It's not only for other people. It's for YOU. No matter who you are, no matter what you have done. Jesus isn't going to freak out on you. He's not going to go into a panic in your storm. He is the same yesterday, today and tomorrow. Jesus is.

Jesus, how many times have I wished for the storms to pass me? How many times have I questioned what was happening in my life? Thank you for reminding me that nothing phases you, that the storm is not a surprise, that you are more powerful than the storm. So often, I have looked like one of the 12, panicking and fearful instead of confident in you. Jesus, I want your calm. I claim that for myself. Holy Spirit, when I feel like I am drowning, let me hold to you, let me look to you. Let me remember that my security is in you and nothing else. Amen.

DAY 19:

What's Keeping You Up At Night?

Then Jesus said to his disciples: "Therefore I tell you, do not worry about your life, what you will eat; or about your body, what you will wear. For life is more than food, and the body more than clothes. Consider the ravens: They do not sow or reap, they have no storeroom or barn; yet God feeds them. And how much more valuable you are than birds! Who of you by worrying can add a single hour to your life? Since you cannot do this very little thing, why do you worry about the rest?"

LUKE 12: 22-26

Worry has to be one of the most human of qualities and probably the one that is most at odds with us created in the image of God. God created us in his image, yet nowhere in the Bible have I ever read that God worries. There are no verses where God is concerned with an outcome. There are no passages where he is up all night playing through all of the "what if" scenarios or trying to figure out a way to "fix things."

And then there's us. Human beings who spend hours worrying. Hours thinking through our marriage from every angle. Googling websites, talking to others, reading everything we can get our hands on. Watching programs about our situation. Trying to figure out a different scenario. Practicing conversations. It's exhausting. It wears us out. It wears out the fabric of our marriage.

I've done this throughout my marriage, and then I remember the rest of this passage: "Who of you can add a single hour to your life...why do you worry about the rest?" Even though you and I have been created in the image of God, we are not God. We cannot add more days to our lives or change the outcome through worrying.

God did not create us to be worriers, he created us to be worshippers. Worry does not change the outcome, worship does. When you and I choose to worry, we start focusing on our ourselves and what we can do in our strength. When you and I choose to worship it puts the focus on what Jesus can do. Do you see the difference?

Your strength or Jesus' power? When you read those words, it seems like a no-brainer doesn't it? And yet, the minute that something goes wrong in our marriage we are immediately drawn to worry. How can I fix this? What does this mean for me? What are the implications for my marriage? What's going to happen?

STOP IT! You aren't helping the situation, in fact, you may be making it worse. Do you realize that you can't make this better by yourself? You can't change the outcome in your strength. We all need Jesus. We need his strength. We need his influence. We need his power. We are so limited in our capacity as humans. We only see our little piece of the world, and we only know what we know.

God knows everything. He knows the next steps. He knows the outcome. Remember Jeremiah 29:11? "For I know the plans I have for you declares the Lord?" You and I need to stop worrying and start getting involved in the process with God. Our marriages need us to seek him, to seek his word.

So often, I'll hear couples in coaching say, "I just wish I knew God's will for my marriage. I wish that I knew what I'm supposed to do. If I could just figure that out, I could stop worrying."

Newsflash: It's easy to know God's will. Open your Bible. God wrote his will for your life on every page. God's will for your marriage is spelled out in the words that fall across the pages.

We worry because we don't know.

We don't know because we don't spend the time.

We don't spend the time because we think that we are too busy.

If worry is consuming your life then you have the time, you just happen to be spending it in an unproductive way. What if you took all the time that you were spending in worry and transferred that to living under God's words, to listening to God?

We don't live that way because we don't think that we matter to God, we believe that we aren't that important to Him. The truth is that you and your marriage are precious to God. You matter. Jesus compares you and me to the ravens in this passage, birds who do nothing, birds who have no capacity to worship their creator, birds who just exist and yet they are provided for. So are YOU!

You were created in God's image with the ability to worship your creator. That ability sets us apart, and that ability gives us an outlet for the energy that we would otherwise spend in worry. Every day you have the opportunity to use your voice, to use your time, to use your actions to worship or to worry. If you choose to worry, you put more distance between you and your spouse and even between you and God. If you choose to worship, you close the gap between you and God, and when that gap gets smaller, the distance between you and your spouse shrinks as well.

It's a choice.

Worry will always lead to disconnect because worry does not involve action. Stop thinking that you don't matter and have to do everything on your own. God has told us that he will always be with us, stop acting like that promise was intended for everyone else but you.

Jesus, I have spent so much time worrying about my marriage. I have felt the need to fix everything, to think that it's all about what I can do in my strength. Funny how my strength is never enough. You are right when you say that I cannot even add an hour to my life. Jesus, I don't want to be a worrier, I want to be a worshipper. I want to turn to you instead of turning to myself. I want to know you and your word so well that I can hold onto your promises instead of feeling like I don't know what the plan is. You've got this, all of it. I need to be in alignment with you always. Amen.

DAY 20:

It's Time to Say Thank You

Now on his way to Jerusalem, Jesus traveled along the border between Samaria and Galilee. As he was going into a village, ten men who had leprosy met him. They stood at a distance and called out in a loud voice, "Jesus, Master, have pity on us!"

When he saw them, he said, "Go, show yourselves to the priests." And as they went, they were cleansed.

One of them, when he saw he was healed, came back, praising God in a loud voice. He threw himself at Jesus' feet and thanked him— and he was a Samaritan.

Jesus asked, "Were not all ten cleansed? Where are the other nine? Has no one returned to give praise to God except this foreigner?" Then he said to him, "Rise and go; your faith has made you well."

LUKE 17:11-19

Leprosy was a horrific disease in Jesus' time. Those with this were considered unclean and cast out. They could have no contact with others who were healthy and formed leper colonies where they could exist with others. Because of this, they had to stand "at a distance" as Jesus came into their vicinity. It was understood that they could not come too close and yet like so many in Jesus' life, they had a sense of the power within him.

These men, who had no contact with others, knew that Jesus could ease their suffering. This knowledge is why they called out and said, "have pity on us." What a humbling moment! Did you notice that Jesus did not get into a long conversation with them? He did not discuss their behavior of what they had done to find themselves in this position. He acknowledged them, sent them on their way and in the process they were cleansed. What happened after is what makes all of the difference.

One man realizes that his life has been changed. He knows that he has been given a gift and he knows who gave it to him. At that moment he makes a decision. He could have been like the others and just continued with his life, ignoring what had been a life-altering change. Instead, he chooses to return to Jesus, to say thank you.

What happens when you say thank you to your spouse? Walls are broken down, a connection is made, hurts are healed. The gift of cleansing, the gift of forgiveness is just that, a gift. It's not something that your spouse has to give you. That's why when they do, it's so important to acknowledge it. Why? Because their gift has forever changed the course of your life. Instead of being cast out by your circumstances you can become a part of the life that you once had. Jesus didn't have to do anything for the lepers. He didn't have to heal them, but he did with no expectations.

Did you notice the words chosen in those two different parts of the story? All of the men were cleansed but only the man who returned to thank Jesus was made well. Being cleansed is temporary, being made well is permanent. Nine men received a change in their circumstances. One man received a change in his entire being. Gratitude creates a permanent shift in the lives of those who express it. When you choose to express gratitude you are acknowledging both the giver and the gift. It is a heart change.

What do you need to acknowledge? What do you need to say thank you for? Our marriages need more gratitude. Our marriages need to hear the words, "Thank you." These words stop us from thinking that it's all about us. They break a cycle of selfishness.

We don't need more temporary changes in our marriages. We need permanent change. Making the decision to express gratitude is what creates that permanent change. Here's a little secret about gratitude, when you choose to express it, you begin to see it appear more often. Your words are powerful, and they create a lasting impact in the lives of those around you, especially your spouse.

Jesus, I want to create permanent change in my marriage. I want us to be made well, not to be simply cleansed. Let my words be words of life, encouragement and gratitude for the things that my spouse does. Holy Spirit, open my eyes to who they are and what they do. I don't want to become numb to my spouse's positive impact on me or our life together. Jesus, I want to respond to the prompting to say thank you for the little things. So often, I have thought, "It's no big deal." The truth is that everything that my spouse does for me is a big deal. I want to be like the man in this passage, stopping and making the time to acknowledge what I have been given. I want to be a person who appreciates my gifts no matter how big or small. One interaction with you changed everything. Let the same be true in my marriage. Amen.

DAY 21:

I Forgive You

Two other men, both criminals, were also led out with him to be executed. When they came to the place called the Skull, they crucified him there, along with the criminals—one on his right, the other on his left. Jesus said, "Father, forgive them, for they do not know what they are doing." And they divided up his clothes by casting lots.

LUKE 23:32-34

Picture yourself in that place, hanging on a cross, mortally wounded, with the lowest of the low on either side of you. Would you have it in you to say, "God, forgive them, they don't know what they are doing"? I don't think that I would and yet, once again Jesus is setting the example for us and how we are to do marriage.

The worst moment of his life, in excruciating pain, and this man asks for forgiveness for you and me. That's powerful.

That's what we are to do in our marriages.

How many times have you made a decision in your marriage not realizing what the consequences would be to your spouse? Not realizing how their feelings would be hurt or how that decision would make them feel. We have all made poor choices. Choices that involve manipulation, deception, lying, cheating, stealing and the list goes on and on. It's the hurtful words said in anger. It's shutting down when the confrontation gets out of hand. It's becoming too friendly with someone else. It's indulging in an addiction that you think is hidden. It's putting everyone else ahead of your spouse.

I did it on a trip to Mardi Gras, three years into our marriage when I was drunk and choose to kiss another man thinking that it was OK because I was "at Mardi Gras." I did it when I overspent hundreds of dollars that we didn't have and thought that I could hide it. I've been the one to make poor decisions, and I've been on the receiving end of them as well.

Our marriage has been far from perfect no matter what it looks like now, no matter what you think based on what you see on social media. We are a couple that continues to be a work in progress.

Human beings hurt other human beings, and it seems that we are much more likely to hurt the ones that we love the most. Maybe it's because we spend so much time with them. Maybe it's because we just expect that they will be around forever. Maybe it's just that we take their feelings for granted and care more about what others think. I don't know why we do it, but we do. Often, I think it's done unconsciously, especially when it becomes more about meeting our own needs than looking to the needs of our spouse.

When Jesus hung on the cross, you and I received an incredible gift. It was a gift that we did not earn. It was a gift that we did not deserve. And yet...it was given to us with no questions asked.

Father forgive them

Jesus hung there on a cross, nails were driven into his hands and feet, a crown of thorns on his head, his back stripped of flesh from the beating he hand received and called out to his Father. He didn't call out and say, "Father, what the *&(*^ is going on?" He didn't cry out and say, "Father, make it stop." He didn't cry out and say, "Father, why are you doing this to me?" All of these are things that I have cried out when life seems horribly unfair, and these are things that maybe you have said yourself.

Instead, Jesus said, "Father forgive them..." He asked for our forgiveness and in those 3 little words, he did not specify the "them". It's not just the criminals, but those that mocked him, beat him, condemned him, turned their back on him, those that couldn't be bothered to take a stand, that took the easy way, that didn't care. He asked for forgiveness for you AND me. He asked for the forgiveness of our sins because he could see, and he understood that now as then,

they do not know what they are doing

We live in a world where our selfishness is encouraged. From selfies to "have it your way"-everything is about me and my desires. It's about what I want when I want it and how I want it. I deserve to be happy, and if I'm not happy, it's time to change the external. The "we" is not encouraged. It's this environment in which we enter into marriage. It's this environment in which we make a lifetime commitment. Lots of times the happiness factor and my selfish needs trump the needs of my spouse and my marriage, without me even thinking about it.

"They do not know what they are doing." Jesus knew. Jesus knew that there were going to be times where we were so focused on our desires that we would be blind to the needs of those around us. He knew that in a world of sin that there would be times where the temptation was so great that we would not stop to consider the consequences of our actions. He knew that we could never know the full implications of what one decision would be in our lives or our marriage. Jesus knew. And he asked for our forgiveness in spite of knowing.

It's time for us to change the words in that statement for the health of our marriage. It's time for a spirit of forgiveness to invade your marriage.

Father, forgive my spouse, for he/she does not know what he/she is doing.

What would your marriage looked like if you practiced forgiveness on a daily basis? Merriam-Webster.com defines forgiveness as:

to stop feeling anger toward or to stop blaming someone

What would your marriage look like without the anger or the

blame? Jesus took away God's anger and God's blame. Isn't it time for us to do that in our marriages? How toxic has it been in your marriage when the anger or the blame has become overwhelming? You don't have to live that way. You don't have to live consumed with anger or blame. You can choose to ask for forgiveness from your spouse. You can decide to practice forgiveness in your marriage.

Forgiveness is not a one-time event. It's not something that you say and then you are done with it. It is something that we as humans need to repeat over and over again.

Jesus, when I think about your body on the cross, broken and beaten, and your ability to ask for forgiveness for me, I am humbled. You could have demanded the angels of Heaven to come and destroy everyone. You could have cried out for yourself, and you didn't. You asked God to forgive me. You demonstrated at that moment that it wasn't about you, it was about your capacity to love. Thank you for showing me that forgiveness is an act of love and not of weakness. Extending forgiveness takes strength that many times I don't feel I have. Jesus, give me the strength to forgive no matter what the hurt is. Give me the willingness to forgive when I want to hold onto the bitterness and the pain. I cast off the spirit of unforgiveness that has invaded my heart and my marriage. I choose to live in love. I choose to follow your example. Amen.

SECTION 4:

YOU ARE NOT TOO BUSY

"I'm so busy." We say this like it's a badge of honor. We say it with pride as if it's the explanation for everything. You know that you've said it and you know that you've heard it from your spouse. The truth is that we are never too busy for the things that we want or the things that matter to us.

We need a shift in our mindset. We need a shift in understanding that what we speak into our lives will come to be. If you are living out this call to love your spouse, you will make different decisions. You will choose to get your priorities in line with Jesus. When you get in alignment with Jesus, your life, your marriage and your tasks will fall into place.

D A Y   2 2 :

Are You Present or Are You Busy?

As Jesus and his disciples were on their way, he came to a village where a woman named Martha opened her home to him. She had a sister called Mary, who sat at the Lord's feet listening to what he said. But Martha was distracted by all the preparations that had to be made. She came to him and asked, "Lord, don't you care that my sister has left me to do the work by myself? Tell her to help me!"

"Martha, Martha," the Lord answered, "you are worried and upset about many things, but few things are needed—or indeed only one. Mary has chosen what is better, and it will not be taken away from her."

LUKE 10: 38-42

Mary and Martha. It's the age old story of being busy versus being present. It's the story of doing vs. being. It's the struggle of every married couple.

There are so many things that need to be done. Between work and the kids and the household chores, you are busy. Add in the family get-togethers, parties, and volunteering, and it's no wonder that so many of us are screaming out like Martha did, "I'm doing all of this by myself. Why isn't anyone helping me?"

I've yelled that to Tony and the kids, as recently as last week. I get so wrapped up in all of the tasks that have to be done, sometimes it's my entire focus, and in the midst of that, I lose out on time being with them. It happens between Tony and me when we get so focused on the next project, the next article, the next podcast that we don't take the time to spend time together. It happens when too many weeks have gone by without a date night. Or too many months without a getaway.

In the busyness, in the midst of all of the tasks that have to get done, what does Jesus say? "...few things are needed...Mary has chosen what is better."

Few things are needed to make our relationships work. It's not about always having clean clothes, clean dishes or even food in the refrigerator. It's not about the cupcakes made for the PTA, the number of hours we have worked, the titles that we have or the people that know us. It's about the relationships that we are investing in, the ones that we are choosing to build.

Look at Mary. She was taking the time to build the relationship with Jesus. She was spending time with him, listening and being with him. It's the same thing that we have to do in our marriages.

You and I can become so busy with all of the things that need to get done. With the way that we are all so connected these days, you are constantly on call. Between email and text messages, someone can reach you at any time, any place. And for most of us, there's the inherent need to respond, to say, "Oh, I have to take care of this. It will only take a minute." Or, "Let me grab this, I shouldn't be long."

Every time, every single time that you make your marriage secondary to someone or something you tell your spouse that they are not important. You tell them, in your actions, that you would rather be busy with others than present with them. As I write these words, I see many images flash in front of my eyes. I see all of the times that I have chosen to stare at a screen instead of staring at Tony. I see all of the times that I have allowed my schedule to overtake our time together. I see all of the times I have, without words, told Tony, "You are not important."

My guess is that you have had at least one experience like this. Let me be clear, I know all of those things are important, and I know that they all have to get done. You would all like to have that magic wand that would make laundry and dishes and the bills and the honey-do list disappear but you don't.

Because you don't have that magic wand, it comes down to how we choose to manage our time and the attitude that we have toward our schedules. Yes, Martha had stuff that had to get done. Yes, there were things that she had chosen to do to make Jesus' stay at their home more enjoyable. However, her complaining and her resentment toward her decisions further complicated her relationship with Mary and with Jesus.

It was her choice to prepare for Jesus in her particular way. It wasn't Mary's choice. It was her choice to be distracted. It wasn't Mary's choice. It was her choice to complain. It wasn't Mary's choice.

What choices are you making in your marriage today?

Are you choosing only to do things one way? Is it your way or the highway?

Are you distracted instead of present?

Are you a complainer?

Think about it. Martha was creating one environment in her home while Mary was creating another. Which would you rather be a part of? Which one had Jesus at the center?

Our marriages don't need another busy person. We need to be more like Mary. We need to make the time to be present. We need to choose to be with our spouses. There will always be tasks for us to do. You will not always get one more minute with your spouse. Give both of you the gift of being present, of being fully engaged. Jesus said, "Mary has chosen what is better, and it will not be taken from her."

Jesus, I get stuck in the busyness trap. I am constantly thinking about all of the things that I need to do. I get stuck in my obligations. I get stuck in the worry. I complain. I yell at my spouse. Jesus, there are so many times that I am Martha in my marriage. I want to be more like Mary. I want to be fully present when the two of us are together. Holy Spirit, make me aware of the times that I am choosing busyness over a connection. I declare today I am no longer a slave to the to-do list. I walk in the freedom of knowing that I will never be disappointed if I choose my marriage first. Thank you for the reminder that in choosing what is better, in choosing relationships, especially my marriage, that this cannot be taken from me. Amen.

DAY 23:

Stop the Glorification of Busy

The apostles gathered around Jesus and reported to him all they had done and taught. Then, because so many people were coming and going that they did not even have a chance to eat, he said to them, "Come with me by yourselves to a quiet place and get some rest."

MARK 6: 30-31

We're doing too much.

We're always plugged in.

We're constantly saying yes.

We're constantly on the move.

Busyness is killing your marriage.

Jesus invited his apostles to come with him to a quiet place and get some rest. He's made that invitation to you as well. At no other time in history have we been more connected to technology, more plugged into media, more exposed, more obligated. And when you look around you, what do you see?

- Loneliness

- Depression

- Addiction

- Heartache

- Disconnect

- Broken relationships

It's time to change how you do marriage. It's time to choose quiet and rest. Your marriage needs downtime. You need the space to refresh and restore yourself. Today more than ever people are complaining of burnout, and they are taking dramatic actions to "fix themselves" or to check out of the relationship (excessive spending, social media, pornography, drugs, alcohol, affairs). The problem is that these actions don't solve the problem, they just create new ones.

Jesus had the answer, "Come with me by yourselves to a quiet place and get some rest."

Come with me

Jesus knows that for our marriages to be healthy we need to spend time with him. We need to read our Bible. You and I need to be in prayer for ourselves, for our spouses and our marriage. When you choose to spend time with Jesus, it will not take away from the time with your spouse. Rather it will equip you for all that marriage and life will throw your way. It's about having Jesus at the center of your life and the center of your marriage. It's about knowing what is a priority for you.

By yourselves

Yes, being in church is important. Yes, being in a small group/home group/connect group is important. However, there are times that you have to be with Jesus by yourself. Just like there are times that you need to be by yourself with your spouse. Jesus didn't tell his apostles to stop hanging out together. He didn't say don't go to church. He didn't say don't go to conferences. He didn't say stop attending worship nights, home group, or prayer meetings. He did say that there needed to be time that we were one-on-one with him. Why? Because restoration isn't found in the crowd, rejuvenation doesn't come from the group. Because you can't know someone if you don't spend time with them. Jesus is modeling the importance of one-on-one time with him, and with our spouses, with this one phrase.

To a quiet place

Our world is so noisy. People walk by you talking on their phones.

The computer, the phone, the TV, the radio, movies, social media, everything, is clamoring for your attention all the time. We live in a world that has seemingly lost an appreciation for the quiet place, for being disconnected from electronics, for just being. It's destroying us and our marriages.

Jesus knew that our lives were going to be noisy. He understood that there were going to be a million and one things clamoring for our attention, so he was intentional when told the 12 to go to a quiet place. Your spirit and mind need quiet. It's in the quiet that we are restored. It's in the quiet that we have time to think. It's in the quiet that we slow down and process what is happening in our lives. The noisy place keeps our marriage living at a surface level, existing but not growing. It's in the quiet place that we have an opportunity to explore our feelings, to become reflective, to deal with our "stuff".

Don't avoid going to the quiet place because it feels scary or uncertain. Make the choice to go to there in order to become the husband or wife that Jesus intended for you to be.

Get some rest

A lot of you just read that one phrase and thought, "That would be so nice." Just a bit of rest, downtime, nothingness-no appointments or commitments for a bit. Busyness is not the prize, it's an avoidance tactic. Staying busy keeps you from feeling, it keeps you from doing, and it keeps you in a constant state of stress.

Your marriage needs you to rest. Your marriage needs you to say no to everything and everyone else so that you can be fully present in your marriage. Your spouse needs you not to be so burned out doing for others that there is nothing for you to give to the marriage. You need to make the choice that you will care for yourself first, that you will seek rest.

God did not tell us to rest because we are weak or because he was punishing us. God gave us rest as a gift. It was part of the perfect plan in the Garden of Eden. If it's part of God's perfect plan, then why are you rejecting it in your life? You need rest, stop fighting it!

Jesus, with open arms, I turn to you and say "Yes, I am ready. I am willing to go with you to the quiet place. I am ready to rest." Jesus, you know that I use busyness as an excuse in my marriage. You know that I use busyness to avoid stressful situations or to avoid working on myself. It's easier to do for everyone else than it is to be quiet and focus on my marriage. I want to be the spouse that has learned that time with you is never wasted time. I want to be the spouse that demonstrates the value that quiet time has in my life and my marriage. I want rest to be a discipline, not a suggestion. Holy Spirit, convict me when I buy into the lies of the world. Open my heart to value what you value, including quiet time. Let me remember that the world will not come to an end if my phone is turned off, if I miss the show, or if I don't check email right this very second. Jesus, I know that in order to strengthen my marriage, to be the best that I can be, it has to start with my relationship with you, spending time in the quiet place with you. Without that, I have nothing. Without that, I am trying to do all things in my own power, instead of relying on you. Amen.

DAY 24:

What Keeps You Distracted?

Then he said to them, "Watch out! Be on your guard against all kinds of greed; life does not consist in an abundance of possessions."

LUKE 12: 15

Usually this passage is preached or discussed in terms of money and finance. It's the passage that so many use when they are warning others not to get so wrapped up in their money or their things. Don't be greedy. When you stop and shift the focus from the material world to the relational word this already powerful conversation takes on a whole new meaning.

Watch out!

We've all yelled this at one time or another, when you are driving down the street, crossing traffic, or putting something hot on the table. Jesus wants us to open our eyes. He wants us to be paying attention because what comes next is so important. He recognizes the fact that he has to get our attention before he can share his insights. There are times when you need to be shaken out of your routine so that you can pay attention.

Be on your guard

How amazing that Jesus takes the time to warn us of the challenges that we will face in this world. He could have left us on our own. He could have told us to figure it out for ourselves. He could have washed his hands of us and said, "You know what, they aren't worth it. These humans are too much trouble. They don't ever seem to learn."

He didn't do that. Up until the moment he died, and even after, Jesus has spoken words into your life and mine, equipping us with tools and knowledge that we can use to make our lives and our relationships better and stronger. This is one of those instructions.

So often in marriage we get complacent. We get to the point where we are just going through the motions. You know what I mean. It's when you find yourself driving somewhere, and you think, "Where am I going and how did I get here?" It's looking at your spouse one day and thinking, "When did we get to this place? How long have we been treating each other like this?"

Be on your guard in your marriage. We need to treat our marriages with intention. We need to be vigilant about protecting our relationship from all attacks. We need to create guardrails to keep us and our marriage safe. The attacks are real, and they don't just happen one time.

against all kinds of greed…

Greed is defined as an intense and selfish desire for something, especially wealth, power, or food. Jesus didn't say that we only need to be concerned about being greedy about money. He said all kinds of greed. Have you ever stopped to think what you might be greedy about?

The money part we know and when it comes to the last french fry or last cookie, we understand that. But what about power? What about time? What about your phone? Where do you see the greed in your marriage?

Your greed can play out in many different ways in your marriage. You can be greedy with the power that you exercise in the bedroom. Are you saying no more than you say yes? Do you withhold sex? Do you have to have everything in your home, in your marriage a certain way? These behaviors are greed in your marriage. This greed destroys the partnership that the two of you have. When you are greedy for power, you take the idea of two become one and make it all about you. You are the only one in the equation. Being power hungry is dangerous because the more power that you insist on, the more power that you receive, the more resentment you create in your marriage. It's not about give and take anymore; it's only about taking.

Are you time greedy? Do you have to fill every minute of every day? Do you insist that you and your spouse spend every moment possible together? Busyness is not all it's cracked up to be. It's a way to avoid quiet and restoration. It's way to stay on the treadmill and never get a break. Or maybe it's not busyness, in your case you are greedy with your spouse's time. You don't want them ever to do anything without you. You want them always with you. You don't want them to have friends. Your time greediness is suffocating your spouse. Your spouse cannot be your everything. They are human and aren't designed to be all things to you. They need to have time away from you. They need to pursue their own interests. Think of it as a way to enhance the relationship as you have more things to share and discuss.

And yes, I am going to bring up the phone. Some of you are greedy about where you are putting your eyes. You want to consume all the information. You want to be up to date on everything, sports, Pinterest, Facebook friends. You are constantly looking outward, wanting more information and more stimulation. And then you have nothing to give your spouse. You don't want to be interrupted. You don't want them to ask you to put your phone down. You're an adult, and you want to be able to do what you want to do. Your greediness to be more involved in other's lives than in your own is destroying your marriage. Your spouse can't keep up with what is flashing through your feed every few seconds.

Life does not consist in an abundance of possessions.

Greed is all about getting more. It's about a selfish desire. You can never acquire so many things that you have enough. There will always be someone who has more. There will always be another level, a bigger prize.

There is nothing wrong with striving to better yourself. The problem comes when your greed for more possessions, more power, more time, comes at the cost of your marriage. Your greed can, and will, destroy your marriage. Becoming aware of it is the first step, the next step is to take action to make your relationships more important than your possessions. Jesus instructed us to watch out for all kinds of greed. Today it's time to work on yourself and begin the process of eliminating greed so that you can make space for love.

Jesus, I'm greedy. I know it, and you know it. It may not be all about material possessions for me, but there are areas of my life where I want more, where I want things my way. Your words spoken here hit me right in the heart. It's so easy for me to look at others with their materials possessions and call them greedy and yet, you are opening my eyes to the ways that I am greedy in my marriage. I have been in this crazy race to have more, get more and yet-at what cost? In these words, I realize that often the cost has been my marriage, my relationship with my spouse. Holy Spirit, I desire freedom from the greed. Open my eyes when I seek my needs instead of those of my spouse. Let me stop when it becomes all about me. I pray for an interruption when I have let my guard down and allowed those other influences to take over my life. Amen.

DAY 25 :

Saying No, the Best Yes You Can Give

Then Jesus was led by the Spirit into the wilderness to be tempted by the devil. After fasting forty days and forty nights, he was hungry. The tempter came to him and said, "If you are the Son of God, tell these stones to become bread."

Jesus answered, "It is written: 'Man shall not live on bread alone, but on every word that comes from the mouth of God.'"

Then the devil took him to the holy city and had him stand on the highest point of the temple. "If you are the Son of God," he said, "throw yourself down. For it is written:

"'He will command his angels concerning you,

and they will lift you up in their hands,

so that you will not strike your foot against a stone.'"

Jesus answered him, "It is also written: 'Do not put the Lord your God to the test.'"

Again, the devil took him to a very high mountain and showed him all the kingdoms of the world and their splendor. "All this I will give you," he said, "if you will bow down and worship me." Jesus said to him, "Away from me, Satan! For it is written: 'Worship the Lord your God, and serve him only.'"

MATTHEW 4:1-10

Wealth and power, creature comforts, stability-who doesn't want this in some form? These are ALL tools that the devil uses to throw us off track, to get us on a detour from the life for which we were designed. Jesus resisted every temptation. He told the devil to take a hike! He saw the temptations and realized that they were a distraction from his mission. You and I need to adopt that same attitude.

Temptations constantly bombard us. Everything from shiny new technology that distracts us from the work that we are supposed to be doing to people that don't have our best interests at heart. From social media that has us comparing ourselves to each other to the lure of the quick dollar. Temptations are EVERYWHERE, and they all look amazing. They look fun. They look exciting.

We live in a world where it has become acceptable to succumb to temptation. In fact, we even use the phrase, "The devil made me do it." It's time to take back the responsibility for our lives and our decisions. Our example, in Jesus, is to say "NO" to temptations. Our example is to remember that the end goal is that we are to "Worship the Lord your God and serve him only." Matthew 4:10

Your marriage and mine do so much better when we are focused on this simple direction. If we remember, on a daily basis, that we are to worship God and serve him only, this will impact every relational decision that we make. When you decide to weigh your temptations against the command to worship God only, you will find what I did. The temptations don't stand up against the direction to worship God and serve him. Why? Because responding to temptations is all about you, worshiping yourself and serving your needs only.

It's hard to see those words in black and white. I like to think that I am not a selfish person but giving into temptation is ALL about being selfish. It's all about me and my needs and what I want. When you choose to resist temptation you are choosing to be selfless in your life. It's the example that we have in Jesus.

Stop for a moment and think this through. Jesus was fully man and fully God. He could have any of those things that Satan presented to him. As the creator of heaven and earth, he had formed the rocks and the ability to make food to meet his needs. As God, he already had the angels at his command. As the creator, the kingdoms of the earth were already his. Satan was not tempting God; he was tempting humanity with the things that to this day continue to cause us to stumble.

By themselves not a single one of these things is evil. Money is not evil, comfort is not evil, status or accomplishments are not evil. The destructive nature comes when we pursue these things above our relationship with God. When the pursuit becomes all about you or all about me, when I decide that I must have these things at whatever price, that is when there is a problem.

The reason that this is such a problem is that when being tempted, we don't stop to count the cost. We don't hear Satan's voice as audibly as Jesus did. We don't see Satan behind these schemes, and yet, in the temptation, Satan is always behind the scenes.

How can I be so sure of that statement?

Because falling into temptation, making selfish choices, choosing yourself over your marriage, these are not actions that bring more life to your relationships. They all lead to darkness. These decisions lead to feeling unworthy, ashamed or guilty. These decisions hurt your marriage instead of helping it. These decisions create lies and secrets. They bring less connection into your marriage instead of more connection. These decisions change the focus from being on the "we" to being all about "me." Selfishness and marriage can only co-exist for a period until the other spouse becomes exhausted with trying to carry both sides of the marriage. Giving into temptation removes you from the place that God designed for you in your marriage, a partner to your spouse.

Satan divides. God unites.

Satan's offerings, in the form of temptation, always have a cost. They are not free. They are not harmless. The temptations offered to you will cost you your self-respect. These temptations will cost you your marriage, your family, your job, your lifestyle, your emotional well-being and even your life.

Jesus' nature is to offer hope. Immediately after being tempted, Jesus provides us with the solution when he says, "Worship the Lord your God and serve him only." It's amazing how many marriages have been transformed by the decision to worship God instead of self. Saying no to temptation is saying yes to God, yes to your marriage, yes to life. It's the ultimate form of worship.

Choosing to worship God and serve him only doesn't mean that you lock yourself up in a room, sing worship songs and pray all day long. Time with God, worshiping and praying, is part of the equation. But worship isn't just the time spent with God. We show how we are worshiping God by how we live our lives.

Serving others is serving God. Putting your spouse's needs ahead of your own is worship. Saying NO to temptations is a form of worship, it's recognizing that easy pleasures or quick gains are not worth the sacrifice of mind, body, and soul. Holding tight to the sanctity of your wedding vows is worship. Worship is how you live your life and how you do your marriage. It's not something that you do for an hour on Sunday. Putting God first is a decision that you make every day. It's a decision that you make even when it would be easier to put yourself first. It's the decision to resist all attempts of the devil to pull you out of your marriage because you know that God's plan for your marriage is beyond your wildest imagination.

Jesus, as I read of your temptation in the desert, I find myself questioning if I would make the same decisions. I know that I have been tempted and have not resisted the devil. I have, throughout my marriage, made decisions that were all about me. Jesus, you know that I struggle with temptation every day. I ask for a greater awareness of these circumstances. I don't want to be blindly responding to what Satan has to offer. Holy Spirit, come and open my eyes. Give me the ability to see what the temptations are and to recognize them as such. Jesus, I know that your strength is within me. I declare that with you, I am strong enough to resist the devil. With you, I am strong enough to say NO to my selfish ways and become selfless in my marriage. Jesus, let my life and how I treat my spouse be worship to you. Amen.

MY THOUGHTS & MY PRAYERS

DAY 26:

Why Are You in Such a Rush?

Now Jesus himself was about thirty years old when he began his ministry...

LUKE 3:23

Sometimes life takes longer than expected. Sometimes preparation is happening, and you don't realize it. In case you missed it, Jesus was born, just like you and me. God came to earth in the form of a baby to show us the importance of preparation and timing. Jesus was not born a carpenter. He was not born as a minister. He did not just start ministering without any preparation. So why does almost everyone think that they can do marriage without any preparation or continued learning? Why do so many think that we should just be able to know what to do in marriage or have it "all figured out." Jesus didn't.

Jesus was born to a carpenter. In those days, the sons often followed in the footsteps of their fathers. Jesus was no exception. He learned the trade from Joseph, practicing, becoming more proficient at the different skills. Think about the little things that Jesus would have had to learn. He had to learn how to level a table without a digital level, how to hammer a nail, how to understand what a customer wanted and then create that very thing. Sound familiar? I bet it does because it sounds a lot like learning about your spouse and your marriage on a daily basis. Jesus, in human form, didn't just "know" how to do these things he had to be taught by those who were more experienced and he had to be willing to learn what he didn't know.

The same is true of marriage.

Being married is a lifelong course in continuing education on your spouse. You did not start marriage knowing everything there was to know about the love of your life no matter what you thought when you said: "I do." Each of us thinks that we know our spouse completely, I mean that's why we agreed to marry them, right? And then sometime after the honeymoon you think to yourself, "Where did this come from?" Or "Who is this person?"

Each of us is changing every day. I have been married for over 20 years and can tell you that the man I married is NOT the man that I am married to today. Physically, it's the same body, although that has changed over the years, emotionally we are 20 years further into this thing called life. He has changed over the years and so have I. The question is this:

Are your continuing to learn who your spouse is or have you stopped?

Just like Jesus wasn't born a carpenter, he also didn't "just start his ministry." There were very specific steps that happened. His presentation in the temple. His teaching in the temple. He collected the 12 disciples and even then he didn't get them all at once. Even though many would point to the changing of water into wine as the "moment" when his ministry started, the truth is every interaction, throughout his life was part of his ministry. Everything that he did prepared him for the next stage of life, it was all about preparing and being ready. This goes for your marriage as well.

Why do you expect more of yourself than Jesus did?

If Jesus needed to prepare and learn even though he was fully God, shouldn't that be a lesson to each one of us? Even though he was fully God, he was also fully human which means that processes and preparation were a part of his life. Why is it so surprising to people that processes and preparation need to be a part of marriage too? As much as I have wished over the years to have a magic marriage wand or fairy dust that I could sprinkle over my marriage I haven't found it. Instead what I have found is that when I am prepared, when I put in the effort to learn, when I become intentional about my marriage I have a much higher rate of success and you do too.

God did not bring Jesus into the world as a full grown man and just plop him into the Middle East and say "GO!". He doesn't do that to you either. However, it's easy to act like that in marriage. We act as if we should already know all that we need to know and not have to work at this relationship. Please get over yourself and your ego, your marriage needs you to move into a place of continuous preparation.

Jesus was 30 years old when he performed his first miracle, when he started the work that God had called him to do. And he only did it for three years. He was in preparation mode most of his life. Why are you stopping after the honeymoon or after a year or two when it gets "hard"? It's critical that you recognize the value of the preparation time, the value in the learning. Just as Jesus, as a man, had to learn and had to prepare, so does each one of us. The wedding isn't the end of the preparation and learning. It's just the beginning.

I was having a conversation with one of the couples that I am coaching the other day and the wife said to me, "My husband is the better spouse. He's always giving 100%. He's always taking care of the details, making sure that we are provided for. He so much better than I am." I stopped her right there because I wanted her to stop beating herself up but more importantly, I wanted her to hear these words,

"You are not supposed to be better than anyone else, comparing yourself to others does not accomplish much except to make you feel less than. You need to be the best YOU that you can be."

That's all God wants from any of us: To be the BEST ME that I can be. God wants us to understand that time in preparation and learning is not wasted time. It's the investment in ourselves and our marriages. It's accepting that the circumstances that you find yourself in over the course of your marriage are going to change you. The person you married on your wedding day has changed over the years. You need to learn who that person is today. Don't skip over learning who your spouse is now, don't see that as time that you can just ignore. That time is one of the most precious gifts that you can give your spouse.

Jesus, thank you for setting the example of preparation and learning. Thank you for demonstrating that the time of preparation is not wasted time. So often, I want to skip over the learning. I want to base everything on the way it used to be. I want to take action NOW. My spouse is not the same as they were and truthfully neither am I. Give me the willingness to invest in learning who they are today. Jesus, you had the armies of heaven at your command, and you did not rush things, you did not change how soon you started performing miracles or how long you ministered. I break off the spirit of impatience with my spouse. I know that my impatience comes from my lack of investment in the relationship, from wanting things to be "my way." Today, and everyday I seek to remember that nothing, nothing is rushed in the kingdom of God, nothing needs to be rushed in my marriage. When I am overwhelmed at what I feel like I don't know about marriage, I have you to remind me that each day is an opportunity to learn more and to invest more in this relationship. Thank you for living a life that I can look to. Amen.

MY THOUGHTS & MY PRAYERS

DAY 27:

There is Rest

"Come to me, all you who are weary and burdened, and I will give you rest."

MATTHEW 11:28

Marriage is hard work. Anyone who tells you differently hasn't been married OR they have just finished their wedding vows and haven't gotten to their honeymoon yet. There are challenges with everything from how the toilet paper rolls (over or under, it does matter) to what to do when you feel the two of you are drifting apart. How you handle it when finances don't go the way you expected or life just seems to be stacked against you.

Hollywood has led us to believe that everything wraps up in a quick 2-hour film with a happy ending. The rest of us live in a world where we are dealing with life with our spouse 24/7. We are dealing with ups and downs, and when things aren't going well we can feel weary or burdened. It can feel like it's all too much. We think to ourselves that things would be better for us if we didn't have to try so hard. We feel like we are the only ones in the world dealing with situations like this.

Have you noticed that Jesus never says, "When things get too hard, why don't you turn to someone else, why don't you shop your concerns away, why don't you have an affair, or start drinking? Why don't you use pornography to satisfy your needs or spend all of your time watching TV or on social media?" I couldn't find any of those alternatives in the Bible, but I do see them everywhere is the world.

Instead, what I did find in the Bible "Come to me...and I will give you rest."

Come to me...

It's an open invitation. Jesus isn't saying come to me between 9-5. He's not telling you that he takes weekends or holidays off. He simply says come to me. He doesn't specify that it's only wives or only husbands. It's not those of you who have never made a mistake or those of you that have been married more than 10 years. He says, "Come to me." That's an invitation for you. No matter where you are, no matter what you have done, no matter what is going on in your marriage, Jesus says, *Come to me.*

- Don't turn to anything else.

- Don't lose yourself in the pleasures of this world to erase or eliminate the challenges of your marriage.

- Don't check out when you are weary.

- Don't give up when it seems to hard.

Come to Jesus. Come to me. This is the same invitation that we should be giving our spouses. Come to me is another opportunity to love them as Jesus does.

all you who are weary and burdened

Jesus knew that things were going to be tough for you. He knew that marriage was not going to look like the Hollywood fairytale all of the time or even most of the time. He knew that you were going to tire out and need help. He knew and yet you you still act surprised that you get tired by this thing called marriage.

It shouldn't be this hard.

Why do we have to work at our marriage?

Why can't it just be easy?

I feel obligated to state the obvious-the fact is that the two of you are imperfect human beings trying to have a perfect marriage. It's going to wear you out. You are going to have seasons where you are tired. There will be times when you can't imagine why getting married was a good idea. I know because I have been there.

I have tried to keep up the facade that everything was ok when it wasn't. I have become exhausted working through the knowledge of pornography in our marriage or dealing with the short sale of our home. I have been tired in my marriage. I have been exhausted to the point that I thought that leaving the marriage, figuratively and literally, was a good idea. It's not.

Why?

Because fatigue is not something new. But how you handle it can be. There is only one person that can "give you rest".

It's what we all long for. Rest from the effort. Rest from the disappointments. Rest from the day to day demands. I've tried to find it in other things. I've had my list of ways to escape the demands of my marriage, trying to find rest and a break from the burden. The problem is that all of those other ways only add to the burden, not reduce it.

Only Jesus can lighten your load and give you the restoration that you are seeking.

How do I know? He has done it for me.

He did it when Tony told me that on business trips, early in our marriage, he would try and pick up women in bars. He did it when I had to share with Tony, that on a trip to Mardi Gras, I had made the choice to kiss other men. He did it when our son Andrew was born at 18 weeks and never took a breath. He did it when we had to short sale our home.

Through decisions that Tony and I made our marriage became a place of exhaustion and weariness. We tried working harder and that didn't work, we were just more tired. We tried running away and that didn't work, our problems always seemed to find us. Things didn't change until we decided to go to Jesus for the rest that we needed. Our lives are not perfect, they are not without challenges, hurts and disappointments. The difference is where we go to find restoration.

We have tried the things of this world and they have done nothing but add to the level of exhaustion. Whatever worldly escape you try will only leave you feeling empty and less connected. It only serves to pull you further away from Jesus AND your spouse.

In Jesus, there is rest. There is hope. There is peace. That's what your marriage needs on a daily basis. In drawing closer to Jesus you create an opportunity to draw closer to your spouse. Don't get caught up in all of the temporary fixes. Go to Jesus. Read his word. Spend time with him. Get to know him. Do life with him. You'll be surprised at the peace that begins to flow through your life and especially into your marriage.

Jesus, your hand is always outstretched in invitation. As I read these words I am struck at how you knew before I was ever married that there would be times that I was tired, times that I was overwhelmed by the adventure of marriage. You knew that I would seek many other ways to find rest and you gave me these words. You gave me you. Holy Spirit, open my eyes to those areas in which I am seeking temporary fixes. Jesus, I break off the need to have a temporary fix, you do not deal in the temporary as you are an everlasting God. You want us to have everlasting restoration and there is only one place where that can be found and that is in you. I am open to correction. I want to turn to you and only to you. Create in me a spirit that seeks you in all times, especially in the hard times. I believe that you are my rest and restoration. Amen.

DAY 28:

Are You Ready?

"Be dressed ready for service and keep your lamps burning, like servants waiting for their master to return from a wedding banquet, so that when he comes and knocks they can immediately open the door for him."

LUKE 12: 35-36

How many times have you said, I want this to happen? I wish that we could do this? It would be great if...? But then an opportunity presents itself and you respond with:

I'm not ready.

When the kids are older, grown or out of the house.

When we have more money.

When we have more time.

There have been many times when I have left the house in the morning to take the kids to school after having just thrown on the quickest things that I can get my hands on, only to run into someone when I am running errands. You know, the day that you spend no time getting yourself ready only to see everyone that you know, or a potential client or even your boss. Or the days when someone says, "Do you want to go grab lunch?" and you're thinking, I'm in my ratty old t-shirt, this is not a good day.

It's the same thing in our marriages. Opportunities are everywhere for connection. The babies are taking a nap. The calendar is miraculously free. Friends offered to take the kids. You got off of work early. You were gifted tickets for a night out. And yet the response is often, "No, not today."

We need to be ready for any opportunity in our marriage. We can't be waiting for the next chance or the perfect timing because it might not come. I have talked to countless men and women, coaching clients, who came to me when their spouses said those fateful words, "I'm done." These men and women were completely baffled because they honestly thought that they had all of the time in the world. They didn't believe that time was running out. They didn't know that they needed to be prepared at all times.

Without attention, your marriage has a finite lifespan. If we are not dressed and ready, both physically and emotionally, we will miss the opportunities that present themselves to us. Jesus doesn't tell us to be dressed and ready because he wants us to always look perfectly put together. He says this because he knows that it's our nature to get complacent about our relationships, especially our marriages.

When the two of you first started dating you were always dressed and ready. You wouldn't have ever thought about showing up wearing old clothes or looking like you just rolled out of bed. Date night was an opportunity to plan, to be ready for anything that might happen. You were always ready to go.

Then you planned for that most wonderful of days, your wedding day. You were dressed and ready for that moment when you would become husband and wife. Then life happened. You got the guy or the girl and being ready and dressed wasn't so important anymore. You stopped trying so hard. You stopped working on the relationship. You stopped being ready for any opportunity to connect with one another.

Newsflash: It's more important to have this connection after the marriage than before. The pre-marriage season might only be a couple of years, but how many years come after the wedding day? For some of you, we are talking about 50-60 years. We need to be dressed and ready for all of those years.

- Being ready means that you are continuing to engage with your spouse.

- Being ready equips you with knowledge about your spouse and what's going on with them.

- Being ready allows you to take action before situations become a problem.

- Being ready means that you aren't a spectator in your marriage rather you are an active participant.

Jesus never expected us to be a spectator. We were always designed to be a participant in this thing called life, especially in our marriages. You and I are uniquely gifted to be the most present person in our spouse's life, if we choose to be. As with everything, it is a choice. In marriage, it is also a gift. If you decide to be ready when opportunities present themselves, you don't ever have to say not now, or I'm not ready. You don't ever have to create a situation where there is a feeling of rejection.

When you are not dressed or not ready, when you push away your spouse with some excuse or another, it's rejection. We live in a world that thinks very little of rejecting people. We have been led to believe that as long as we are happy, or not inconvenienced, then it doesn't matter about anyone else. That is not true in marriage. Our marriages need to be placed where we strive to find opportunities to connect instead of reject. There are plenty of forces pushing down your spouse, don't be another one.

Jesus, I'm ready. I'm ready to do the work it takes to make my marriage extraordinary. I'm willing to change what I need to change. I'm willing to take the action that I need to take. Jesus, I've sat on the sidelines for so long waiting for something to happen, and now I realize that I AM the one to make it happen. Jesus, I know that being ready is a function of being in a relationship with you, that by myself nothing will happen. I'm reminded of the words of Paul in the letter to the Philippians; I can do all things through Christ who strengthens me.(Philippians 4:13) My lack of readiness has been because I have been trying to do it in my strength. I can't do it by myself. I can't do it my way. Jesus, I'm ready to do it your way. Jesus, I'm ready for my marriage to look the way you want it to. Lead my marriage, Jesus. I'm ready. Amen.

SECTION 5:

START WITH THE BABY STEPS

Oh, how we want to run to the finish line. We want to be at that place where everything is good, where we have everything all figured out and life is perfect. I know I have wished for all of the answers, wished that I didn't have to learn <u>so</u> much and yet...

Think about a baby learning how to walk. They aren't born with the ability to run around the house, thank God! Babies have to learn how to hold their heads up, how to roll over, how to sit up, how to pull themselves up and how to move one foot in front of the other. They do this, and then they often fall-a lot!

That's a perfect image of us in our marriages. We have to learn one step before we can take the next one. We make mistakes. We fall down. We figure out how to get back up. The call to love, is a call to keep trying, it's a call to take baby steps every day of your marriage.

DAY 29:

It's Time to Rise

Now there is in Jerusalem near the Sheep Gate a pool, which in Aramaic is called Bethesda and which is surrounded by five covered colonnades. Here a great number of disabled people used to lie— the blind, the lame, the paralyzed. One who was there had been an invalid for thirty-eight years. When Jesus saw him lying there and learned that he had been in this condition for a long time, he asked him, "Do you want to get well?"

"Sir," the invalid replied, "I have no one to help me into the pool when the water is stirred. While I am trying to get in, someone else goes down ahead of me."

Then Jesus said to him, "Get up! Pick up your mat and walk." At once the man was cured; he picked up his mat and walked.

JOHN 5:2-9

We all know couples who are struggling in their marriages. They are sick of what is going on in their relationship. They are blind to the changes that need to be made. They are lame emotionally because of the baggage that they keep carrying around. They are paralyzed with fear. And yet, they keep hoping. They keep waiting for that miracle to happen. Just like in this parable, they are waiting for God to stir the waters so that they can receive their healing.

Did you notice that there was "a great number" of people waiting? I don't know what a "great number" is to you, but no matter how you translate it, it sounds like a lot. All of these people were waiting for the one miracle that came when the angel stirred the waters. This crowd was doing nothing but laying around the pool. They were not trying to work on themselves. They were not taking action. They were only waiting.

Just like a lot of people are waiting when their marriage is not going the way that they anticipated.

"I will wait right here, God, until you fix this."

"I'm waiting on you, God."

"Whenever you are ready, I'll be here."

Nothing happens in your marriage when all you are doing is waiting. Nothing happens when you are waiting for someone else to make a change. Nothing happens when you expect someone else to work your miracle.

This man was waiting for 38 years when he encountered Jesus. Even though Jesus knew, it's interesting that Jesus never asked him, for our benefit, "What is wrong with you? Or "How long have you been here?" These are the questions I think that I would have asked. Jesus is telling us that the condition we are in doesn't matter and it doesn't matter how long we have been like that.

Jesus only asks, "Do you want to be made well?"

Do you want it?

Do you want life to be different?

Do you want to change?

It is only after Jesus asks if he wants to be made well, that we learn that this man has attempted to create change. What starts off sounding like an excuse, "I have no one to put me in the pool." (My healing is dependent on other people.) Changes into his actual need, "While I am coming, another steps into the water before me." (Yes, I want this, I am struggling to do it on my own). For this man, it comes down to the fact that he couldn't do it on his own and he had no one else to help him. For 38 years! When you read his words, you can hear the desperation, the desire for change, the fact that he is still trying to hold onto hope in spite of all of the disappointments of the last four decades.

For this man, the answer to Jesus' question is, "Yes, I do want to be made well. I realize that I cannot do it by myself."

What would it look like if you were this man and your marriage had been in trouble for a very long time? Would you or are you even looking for healing? Are you close but not close enough? Have you been frustrated by things not happening fast enough for you?

Do you want yourself and your marriage to be made well?

It's a legitimate question. There are a lot of people in bad places in their marriage who do not want to get well. They enjoy being miserable. They feel like they are thriving in the "look at me, I'm so pathetic" world. The miracle is right in front of them but they choose to do nothing about it, they choose not to take action.

Do you want yourself and your marriage to be made well? Do you? Are you ready for your healing? Are you willing to take up your mat and walk?

I think that if you have made it this far in the book that the answer is most likely a YES. You have been spending this time building your relationship with God, praying over your life and your marriage, asking God to open your eyes to your role in your marriage. It's time.

It's time to invite Jesus into <u>all</u> areas of your marriage.

It's time to take responsibility for your role in your healing.

It's time to be accountable for what you can do.

It's time for life to be different.

It's time for your encounter with Jesus.

He's telling you to take up your mat and walk. This is going to mean something different for each one of you, but ultimately it means the same to each of you. It's time for you to be healthy, for you to be whole. Your involvement, your action in God's plan for your life, creates powerful transformation. You must be a part of the process.

Jesus, seven little words made all the difference in this man's life, and it's the same seven words that you give each of us. Do you want to be made well? My answer is YES! Holy Spirit, I invite you into all areas of my marriage, not just the ones that are going well. Just like this man acknowledged that he could not do it by himself. I stand before you today and say I cannot do my marriage by myself. My marriage has my finger-prints all over it, and mine are dirty. I need your touch, Jesus. I need a word from you. I need direction. No longer will my ears be shut to you and your commands. I choose to listen to your words. You told this man to, "Get up and walk." I am ready, Jesus. I want to experience health in my marriage. I come before you with my heart laid out, with all of the problems that we are having, with all of the ways that I have tried to do things on my own. Jesus, tell me what to do and today I will listen. Amen.

DAY 30:

Are You Working Your Own Field?

Then he said to his disciples, "The harvest is plentiful but the workers are few."

MATTHEW 9:37

I want a marriage where we are best friends.

I want to be happy.

I want us to live a fairytale.

I want us to make an impact.

I want us to have an incredible connection, an amazing sex life, the kind of marriage that everyone admires.

I want to have the kids, the house, the dream.

You have probably said something like this at some point in your marriage. Maybe you've even said most of these in some way, shape or form. We know what we want but are we willing to do what it takes to get there?

If you have ever seen farmlands, you know that they stretch as far as the eye can see, crops in every direction. Between farm machines and the workers much can be accomplished in harvesting the crop. Without someone to do the work of the harvest, the crop sits in the field and dies. It takes everyone doing their part to have a successful year.

The same is true in your marriage. In your marriage there is you and your spouse, you are the workers. The two of you are the ones working the crop which is your marriage. What you do today matters to the harvest. How you speak to your spouse, what actions do you, what decisions do you make, each of these matter. You are the workers. Are you both engaged in bringing in the harvest?

These are hard questions. I promised at the beginning of this book that I would be honest. So the truth is that there have been many seasons in our marriage when I have not been engaged in the harvest, when I have not labored in my own marriage, when I have said to Tony (either in words or my actions) "You do all the work."

You know that your marriage doesn't work if you aren't both working. Yes, there are times when you carry the burden for each other but one person cannot do all of the work for the life of the marriage. Marriage is two people coming together. That means that both of you have to labor in the relationship, you have to work for the harvest. You have to be involved in the process. You have to plant seeds in each other and the relationship. You have to invest emotionally in the growth. You have to tend the seeds, nurturing them to yield a full crop. If neither of you is working on the marriage, it withers and dies. If only one of you is working for an extended period, your marriage will not be as fruitful as it could be.

Your marriage needs all of the workers because the harvest is plentiful.

Before the crop can grow, the seeds have to be planted. What you plant is what you get. Your words and your actions are seeds planted into your marriage. Everything that you plant in your marriage will grow into a harvest. Some of it you want, some of it you don't. That's why the workers need to be diligent. The workers need to tend those things that will reap growth and weed out those things that won't.

Your harvest is coming. It's being prepared for you as the two of you work on your marriage. Now is not the time to get distracted by other people's harvests. Do not compare your harvest to what you see on Facebook or Instagram or Pinterest. Your harvest is the result of your efforts. Jesus tells us that the harvest is plentiful but it [your marriage] needs workers [you and your spouse]. Those two things are dependent on each other. You cannot have one without the other.

Many people want the harvest without the work. A harvest in your marriage simply doesn't happen without the work.

This does not mean that the two of you will labor in the same way. Tony and I are very different. We have different skills that we bring to the marriage. Different ways that we see the world. Different ways that we grow and invest in one another. This is not right or wrong, only different.

The harvest needs workers with different skills. You and your spouse are uniquely gifted to handle life in a certain way. In working with your strengths, you will see the harvest come in. You will see growth in all areas of your lives. You will see your harvest reach heights you never imagined.

Your harvest is there. Can you imagine the field of corn, full and ripe at the end of the season? Jesus' word tells us that yours is there. It's not an empty promise. It's not just words on a page. Jesus is telling you that it is there for you and your marriage. It simply needs enough workers to bring in the harvest. Stop waiting for someone else to reap your harvest. Labor in your field and watch it grow.

Jesus, I know that there have been so many times, I have waited for my spouse to do the work. I have been able to see the harvest, but I have sat back and said, "Someone else can do it. I don't want to work that hard. I don't want to get my hands dirty." I have stepped out of the harvest that you have given me. Jesus, today I declare that I am going to work my own field. I am going after the harvest that you have prepared for me. I know that as a team, my spouse and I can accomplish so much together. I can see the seeds that you have planted in our marriage. I want us to be a couple that is diligent about weeding the negatives and encouraging the positives. I understand that what we plant, good and bad, will grow and that by choosing to be active in the work that needs to be done we can have that full harvest. That harvest of more than enough. Amen.

DAY 31:

Just One Touch

As Jesus was on his way, the crowds almost crushed him. And a woman was there who had been subject to bleeding for twelve years, but no one could heal her. She came up behind him and touched the edge of his cloak, and immediately her bleeding stopped.

"Who touched me?" Jesus asked.

When they all denied it, Peter said, "Master, the people are crowding and pressing against you."

But Jesus said, "Someone touched me; I know that power has gone out from me."

Then the woman, seeing that she could not go unnoticed, came trembling and fell at his feet. In the presence of all the people, she told why she had touched him and how she had been instantly healed. Then he said to her, "Daughter, your faith has healed you. Go in peace."

LUKE 8:42-48

Jesus asked, in the middle of a crowd, Who touched me? Who did something to change the situation here? Who took action? Just like it did for this woman, empowerment comes to you when you decide to take action.

The woman in this story had been dealing with a painful situation for 12 years. It was not just painful but embarrassing. The situation made her an outcast. She was considered unclean. These thoughts sound a lot like how you might feel after a revelation of infidelity, financial ruin or anything else you might want to keep a secret.

We feel less than others. We feel embarrassed. We feel cast out.

This woman had been in this situation for 12 years. In spite of living like this for such a long time, she hadn't given up hope that there was a solution. Not only did she have hope BUT (and yes, this is a BIG BUT) she took action. She believed that her circumstances could be different, she thought that her future could be different, so she stepped out of her comfort zone and encountered Jesus.

So many times in your marriage I'm sure that you, just like me, have felt hopeless. What's happening with our finances? What's going on with our kids? Why aren't we connecting anymore? What's wrong with us? All thoughts that are pretty common in marriage and yet they are all questions of hopelessness. How do I know that these are hopeless? Because they almost always get the same response-"I don't know."

"I don't know" is the ultimate statement of hopelessness. This hopelessness can lead to feelings of paralysis. The sense of shame and isolation because of the problems in your marriage have you saying things like:

I can't do anything right.

This situation is never going to change.

How could we ever fix this?

I wonder if you have it in you to be like this woman. If you have it in you to believe, in spite of everything that you have seen and experienced, that things can be different? I wonder if you are willing to encounter Jesus again? I've witnessed the miraculous happen when not only hope but Jesus come into a marriage. Hope is the first step. Jesus is the finish line.

The Bible is full of examples of people, who just like this woman, dealt with challenges for extended periods of time: the blind man, the demon-possessed man, the crippled man lowered through the roof, the leper, and the list goes on. Virtually all of Jesus' encounters were with people who had been struggling with something for a significant period of time. Just like YOU. Coincidence? I don't think so!

You haven't gotten to this place in your marriage overnight. It's been a journey there, and it's going to be a journey to get back to a place of healing.

How remarkable the woman in this story is, in spite of her intense embarrassment and shame, she had incredible faith that just a touch of his robe would be enough. She hoped to move the mountains in her life. She believed with such firm conviction that life could be different, that she continued to try. This is the attitude you need to have in your marriage. Instead of shrinking back from the problems the two of you have you need to be saying to yourself, "It doesn't matter how long this has been a problem, I haven't given up yet, and I'm not going to give up now."

This woman didn't wait to feel better to reach out to Jesus. She didn't wait to be ok to be in his presence. She took action and then experienced healing. How many of you are waiting to feel better about your marriage, or your spouse, before you take action? This woman's interaction with Jesus is a prime example that we have to take action for our feelings to change; not wait for our feelings to change before we can take action.

Stop being ruled by your emotions. They are temporary. They are fickle. They are a roller coaster. If you want your feelings to change in your marriage, reach out and do something about it. Do what you CAN do. You feel hopeless, do something. You wonder if things will ever get better, do something. So often you will find yourself stuck in your marriage not because of doing too much but rather because you are doing too little, waiting for someone or something else to move.

Jesus, there have been so many times that I have chosen to stay stuck in the problem, to have my own pity party. At times, I have been over-whelmed with a feeling of hopelessness. So often I have had the thought that things will never get better, that this situation cannot be fixed. Jesus, I pray for strength to step out of my comfort zone to create a connection first with you and then with my spouse. I declare freedom from the fears that have kept me in bondage, that have kept me from reaching out to my spouse to create a connection with them. Jesus, I no longer want to live a life of pain and misery. I'm asking for the strength to reach out, to come to you when the situation feels hopeless, when I feel lost. Like this woman, I pray to understand that in taking action, everything can and will change. Amen.

DAY 32:

What Are You Asking For?

"So I say to you: Ask and it will be given to you; seek and you will find; knock and the door will be opened to you. For everyone who asks receives; the one who seeks finds; and to the one who knocks, the door will be opened."

LUKE 11: 9-10

Ask, and it will be given to you.

I wonder how many of us have stopped asking in our marriages. It sounds like a silly question but I have to ask it.

Do you ask for things in your marriage or do you demand things be done?

Do you ask for what you need or do you expect that your spouse just knows what you need?

There are a lot of people out there who are expecting things to be given to them without them asking. They are hoping to receive without voicing their needs. They are expecting their spouses to have ESP and the truth is that your spouse cannot read your mind.

Tony and I have been married over 20 years and I will tell you that the times when it seems like we are on the same page or are reading each other's minds, I have to remind myself that it's not ESP, it's just making guesses based on past behavior. Any time that we are in sync, it's more coincidence than actual mind reading. Expecting your spouse to know what's going through your mind is a waste of time for you and a sure way to create frustration in your marriage.

Jesus says ask and it will be given to you. He didn't say demand and it will be given to you. He didn't say hint at it, and you will receive it. He said to ask. I know that over the years I have struggled with this. It's hard for me to ask for help or for what I need. I think to myself, "I should be able to do this on my own. I don't want to ask for help. I don't need somebody else to do it."

The fact is that if you could do everything by yourself, then there is absolutely no need for you to be married. God gave you the gift of your spouse because you cannot be or do all things on your own. It takes you asking for what you cannot do on your own for those things to happen.

"Ask and it shall be given to you."

I think that many people struggle with "the ask."

- What do I ask for?

- How do I ask?

- I don't know if I believe that I will receive what I ask for?

- How long will it take?

- What if I don't get what I asked for?

- What about all of those times that I have asked and not gotten any response?

I will tell you honestly that you will not always receive what you ask for in the way that you ask for it and when you have asked for it. Why? Because we often don't know what is best for us.

Think about a three-year-old that goes into the store and wants this toy and that book and then candy in the checkout line. Most parents choose to say no to some of that or all that. Why? Because they have a greater understanding of what is in the best interests of the child. They know that getting everything at once, while it is fun, doesn't teach the child how to develop patience. Parents know what is coming in a child's life and when would be a good time to provide treats. It's not to say that the child won't receive the gifts but often not in the way or at the time that they wished.

The same is true of what we ask from God. God loves you. God wants to give you the desires of your heart. God wants his children to be happy. However, receiving everything that we want, when we want it, in the way that we want it is not always in our best interests.

Did you notice that Jesus did not say when we would receive?

He didn't say, " Ask, and you will get it right away." He didn't say, "Ask and wait for a week and it will happen." Jesus didn't give you, or me, any time frame on what we would receive or how we would receive it. He only said, "Ask." This command means that you and I have the opportunity to ask knowing that we will receive.

There are times that we have to grow into a space to receive. What we ask for is not always what we are ready for. There are times that what we ask for involves others and they need to be ready for that as well. Our asks are never just about us. We live in an interconnected world and the granting of any request involves many people.

When you ask for something in your marriage or for your marriage, it's not just about you. It's a situation that involves both you and your spouse and kids if you have them. Each of you is on a journey to bring glory to God. It's not about just getting what you ask for. It's not about just giving into your feelings right now. It's about bringing glory to God.

When you and I start to realize that our asks, come with a responsibility to bring glory to God, then the delay is not as hard to handle. We become more capable of understanding that the answer, the gift may look different than what we had imagined. Just like the parent of the three-year-old wanting everything in the store, the parent who knows what is best for the child, your Father knows what is best for you. A delay is not God's punishment. A different answer is not God's denial.

Jesus promises that those who ask will receive and that those who knock will have the door opened. That is a promise for every single one of you reading these words right now. Go ahead and ask. Go ahead and knock. Your Father is there and is waiting to hear from you.

Jesus, so many times I have felt like you didn't care about me or see me because my requests have gone unanswered. If I'm honest with myself, so many times I have asked you for a quick fix instead of true healing. I have wanted the pain just to disappear or things to magically be different. Even as I look at these words, I realize that's not you. You deal in transformation, not magic tricks. Thank you for the promise that what I ask for I will receive. It is my humanity that limits me. It is my past disappointments that keep me from asking. Jesus, I want to be able to ask you for anything and be content in the answers that I receive. Holy Spirit, prompt me to ask. Create in me a heart filled with expectation that what I ask for will happen, in whatever way it is supposed to. Jesus, I don't want to get hung up on the details, I want to remember at all times that everything is designed to bring you glory. Let my responses always point to you. Amen.

DAY 33:

There Are Times to Hold Your Tongue

When he was accused by the chief priests and the elders, he gave no answer. Then Pilate asked him, "Don't you hear the testimony they are bringing against you?" But Jesus made no reply, not even to a single charge—to the great amazement of the governor.

MATTHEW 27: 12-14

Jesus did not speak a single negative word when he accused, when people were speaking poorly of him, when they were calling for his death. He didn't go to their level. He didn't allow them to create an emotional response in him.

I think that Jesus was deeply grieved by what he was experiencing, but he also knew that each of these people had a choice to make and they had made it. They had chosen to go along with the crowd, to get wrapped up in what everyone else was doing. Even to Pilate who didn't agree, but didn't feel he had the ability to go against the crowd, and he turned Jesus over for crucifixion.

I know I would have yelled out.

I know that I would have defended myself.

I know that I would have made my case and repeated it over and over again until I was either hoarse or someone believed me.

How do I know? This same scenario has played out in my marriage.

There have been times when, through a misunderstanding or miscommunication, I have been accused of something that I didn't do. My indignation at this "false accusation" pushed all of my emotional buttons and before you know it, it's like World War 3 in our living room or the car of wherever we are having a conversation. In these instances I have chosen to push my point, to scream as loud as I can or even punish (yes, I'm talking about the silent treatment) those who are bringing words against me, namely Tony.

As I read these words describing Jesus, I don't see any of that behavior. All of those times that I have felt that my actions and reactions were justified don't match up with the example of Jesus.

Jesus knew that the crowd was in a frenzy. He was aware that they were past the point of reason. How many times have I realized that Tony is upset but kept pushing the conversation? How many times have I realized that there's something that he's dealing with and, while I know that it's something that he has to work through, I've still jumped in with both feet to make the situation worse? I think of all of those times when choosing not to engage might have been the best thing for my marriage. Times, when acting like Jesus and allowing him to blow off steam, might have ended the argument or discussion sooner and easier than me having to be right, having to prove my point. Nothing is gained in those situations except hurt feelings and resentment. These are two things that our marriages do not need more of.

There have also been times when I have been on the other side as well. Times when I have been in a frenzy, when everything said to me has just escalated the situation. Times when I have been completely unreasonable and irritated that Tony is acting like Jesus. In those moments he chooses not to engage with me, he chooses to let me work through whatever I have to work through.

Sometimes it's hard to be like Jesus, other times it's hard to receive someone else acting like Jesus.

Our marriages need both. It's so important that you are both striving to be like Jesus because the reality is that you are not always going to pull it off. There will be times when only one of you gets it right or times when neither of you gets it right. The important thing is that you don't stop trying, you don't stop asking yourself that phrase that we've seen everywhere from wristbands to t-shirts. WWJD...What Would Jesus Do?

The phrase might be a little overplayed, but the sentiment isn't.

Our marriages need us to constantly be asking ourselves, what would Jesus do in this situation? If this is one of those times that Jesus would be quiet, I need to be quiet. If this is one of those times that Jesus would let someone vent, I need to let that someone (my spouse) vent. If this is one of those times that I see that my words aren't going to have an impact because my spouse isn't in a place to listen, I must choose silence.

None of these behaviors are accidental. They aren't done to punish your spouse. They are done intentionally with the expectation of growing the relationship.

Nothing would have been gained by Jesus trying to change the crowd's mind and in some respects, even more, would have been lost. Jesus choosing not to act was something that those in the crowd would be able to reflect on, maybe not at the moment, but when things had calmed down. You and I have that same option. We have the same opportunity to reflect on our behavior or on the behavior of our spouse to question where we need to act like Jesus.

I know when Tony looks at me there are many times when he sees Jesus, and many times when he doesn't. Just like you, I am a work in progress, and just like you, I want there to be more times that my spouse sees Jesus than not. Keeping Jesus as your example will impact how you react, there's no way that his example cannot impact you and your marriage.

Jesus, how did you do it? How did you keep calm in the midst of that crowd? How did you choose silence over defending yourself or striking everyone down? I think of you and realize that I still have a long way to go.

Thank you for the example of your life. Thank you for the reminder that I don't have to participate in every argument or fight, that there are times when I can choose silence, and it is the best choice. Holy Spirit, open my eyes and my heart so that I am better able to choose those reactions that point toward you. I know that there are many days when my reactions point more towards me than you. Today, I say that this is the day that I choose Jesus' model instead of my own, Jesus' reactions over my own. Amen.

DAY 34 :

There Are No Insignificant Actions

Late in the afternoon the Twelve came to him and said, "Send the crowd away so they can go to the surrounding villages and countryside and find food and lodging, because we are in a remote place here."

He replied, "You give them something to eat."

They answered, "We have only five loaves of bread and two fish— unless we go and buy food for all this crowd." (About five thousand men were there.)

But he said to his disciples, "Have them sit down in groups of about fifty each." The disciples did so, and everyone sat down. Taking the five loaves and the two fish and looking up to heaven, he gave thanks and broke them. Then he gave them to the disciples to distribute to the people. They all ate and were satisfied, and the disciples picked up twelve basketfuls of broken pieces that were left over.

LUKE 9: 12-17

Imagine being at a concert or sports event where there are tens of thousands of people and no concession stands. You brought some food but ate it on the drive, expecting that there would be somewhere to eat. Here you are with all of these people and there's nothing. Nothing until this random guy takes a few pieces of bread and fish and makes enough food to feed everyone with food leftover. Unbelievable, maybe. Incredible, you bet!

The same thing happens in your marriage and mine every single day. We work with what we have to make something bigger and better than it was on its own.

- We take a few leftovers and whip up dinner.

- We take the money left at the end of the month and figure out a way to pay all of our bills.

- We take 60 minutes and make it into a great date.

- We take two very different people and make a life together.

- We take something that seems so little and make it into something that no one could have ever expected.

Just like Jesus.

We have become a society where everybody wants to see the incredible display of power or influence, right? We want to see the incredible transformation. We think we need to have or be something larger than life to accomplish great things in our marriage and yet...Jesus took five loaves of bread and two fish. Bread and fish. On the surface these items just seem ordinary, they were readily available and yet they weren't even enough to feed a family.

With God, they became the extraordinary. They became more than enough. They met everyone's needs.

You and I need to stop looking for the prize and start working with what we have right in front of us. It begins with the person who faces you in the mirror. Jesus first told the disciples to do something, knowing what their objections were going to be: "We don't have enough." "We can't do this." Sounds pretty similar to what you say to your spouse when things are difficult. "I can't do this." "I don't want to." "I don't know how." Then, as Jesus always does, he set the example.

He took a small lunch and used it to feed thousands. What seemed small made a huge difference. The same idea is true in your marriage.

You have words that you can use to shift the atmosphere.

You have actions that, when done consistently, increase the trust level in your relationship.

You have gifts that are uniquely yours that are a blessing to your spouse.

You have time to give to your spouse.

Each of these words, actions, gifts and time, multiply just like the loaves and fishes. This story of Jesus is so impactful because he didn't just snap his fingers and make a full buffet appear in the middle of nowhere. He didn't come with a caravan of chefs and waiters knowing that there were going to be multitudes. He didn't have food trucks or drive-thrus. He didn't wish for food to drop out of the sky or complain about the circumstances. He didn't blame the disciples for being unprepared. He saw a need and he met it.

Your spouse has needs that you can meet. Needs that are not beyond your capabilities. Needs that you don't have to complain about or wish away. Needs that you, just like Jesus, are uniquely qualified to meet.

What are you waiting for? Jesus didn't wait until there was a crisis. He didn't wait until the crowd was shouting and fighting. He anticipated what was coming and took a proactive approach to solving the problem.

So often, in marriage, there is this "wait and see" attitude. Let me wait and see if this becomes an issue for my spouse. What if we started acting more like Jesus? Instead of waiting for a problem, we look at the circumstances and say, "Let me meet this need now. Let me take what I have and make it a gift for my spouse."

Being proactive is a gift for both of you. It minimizes the stress in your marriage. It meets needs before they become issues. It's leading with a servant's heart in the same way that Jesus did.

Jesus, when I look at the miracles you performed, I am blown away at how simple they seem and at the same time how incredible. Bread and fish. That's it. That's all it took to meet the needs of those around you. Jesus, so often I am looking for the super-duper miracle cure. The one thing that will fix everything but it's not about having one thing. It's about knowing the ONE, You. Jesus, let me daily remember that I have the ability to work with what I have to transform my marriage. The ordinary is extraordinary when brought before you to serve my spouse. I want to be like you, Jesus, not waiting or expecting others to do what I can do, but taking action to get done what needs to get done. Holy Spirit, open my eyes to the ordinary and the opportunities to take action. Let me see in it all of the possibilities that you see. I no longer want to be limited by these self-made ceilings. Let me see and experience all the opportunities to love on my spouse and serve them in the same way that you served the thousands here. Amen.

DAY 35

Leadership Comes Through Service, Not Demands

Jesus knew that the Father had put all things under his power, and that he had come from God and was returning to God; so he got up from the meal, took off his outer clothing, and wrapped a towel around his waist. After that, he poured water into a basin and began to wash his disciples' feet, drying them with the towel that was wrapped around him.

JOHN 13:3-5

Jesus knew exactly who He was. He knew what was coming. He knew the hearts of each of these men who surrounded him, especially Judas who would betray him. Jesus knew and he still he took off his robe and washed the feet of these men.

In the first century, men and women wore sandals and walked around on dusty roads. Their feet would have been filthy. Typically the task of washing the guest's feet would have been the job of a household servant, someone who had no power, someone who was considered unworthy. And yet, what do we see? Jesus is washing their feet. Jesus who just a few days prior had ridden into Jerusalem to the crowd cheering,

"Hosanna!

'Blessed is He who comes in the name of the Lord!' The King of Israel!"

John 12:13

In the course of a few days, he had gone from being cheered as the long awaited Messiah to washing dirty feet. Why would this happen?

Why would Jesus do this?

Jesus was showing us that leadership, in all areas of our lives and especially in our marriage, begins in service. Jesus washed dirty feet. He didn't complain. He didn't say that it was someone else's job. Jesus did what needed to be done.

There is a huge difference between serving from a sense of obligation versus a feeling of love. What have you chosen in your marriage to this point? This verse doesn't say that this was on his to-do list for the day or that he "had to get it done". John says that he loved them to the end and he began to wash their feet. He acted out of love knowing what was coming, knowing that he was about to face the worst days of his life. He knew, and he still served those closest to him.

And then there's me. I get irritated if I walk into the kitchen and have to throw away something left on the counter or if I am interrupted by something that Tony asks me to do. Over the years I've heard many couples complain about everything from having to take out the garbage to having sex with one another.

How does that look like Jesus?

Jesus wasn't too good, too busy, too in charge to get his hands dirty and show love to those closest to him. We shouldn't be either.

So much restoration can happen in your marriage when you remember, and act on, the idea that your highest calling is in serving others, especially your spouse. When you choose to bring an atmosphere of service into your marriage and meet your spouse's needs. When you aren't afraid to get your hands dirty.

It's more than just the act of serving. It's so significant that Jesus chose to take off his regular garments, gathered a towel and girded himself before kneeling to wash their feet. Jesus removed what made him like all of the other disciples in appearance and set himself apart. He did what was necessary to be more efficient at serving. Jesus didn't complain about the obstacles. He didn't use his regular clothes as an excuse. He set himself up to be successful at what he was about to do. There was no huffing and puffing. There was no huge sigh, as if he was frustrated, at having to do ONE MORE THING to demonstrate to the disciples this idea of serving. He transformed himself willingly into a servant and just did it.

Serving without fanfare. Serving without saying, "Hey, look at me, look at what I am doing for you. Hey, do you see what I am doing? Make sure you pay attention because I am doing something for YOU."

None of that.

However, when I look at my marriage, I can think of countless times that I have said to Tony, "Did you see what I did today?" Or, "Just so you know, I took care of X, Y, and Z for you today." Jesus served his disciples with no expectation that they would reciprocate. He knew that they were about to betray him, not just by turning him over to the authorities, but also by falling asleep in the Garden and denying that they knew him. He knew he wasn't going to get anything from them and he still served them.

Serving in my marriage often seems to come with strings attached, with a desire for acknowledgment. Serving your spouse with strings attached, that's the model of the world, that's not Jesus' example. Waiting for your spouse to do for you before you do for them, that's the model that the world lives by. And yet, that's not the model that we have.

That's not who Jesus is.

We need to stop looking at serving our spouse from the eyes of the world and look at them through the eyes of Jesus. Serving needs to be with no strings attached. Serving needs to be a gift that we give because of the love in our hearts, not because of the to-do list.

When you change your perspective, you will see an incredible transformation in your marriage, in your life and in that of your spouse.

When you willingly choose to serve your spouse with no expectations, you become free. Free of disappointment. Free of resentment. Free to love the way that Jesus did. Your spouse experiences the freedom that comes from being loved just the way that they are. It's powerful.

Jesus, I want to serve my spouse the way that you served your disciples. Take away my need for acknowledgment and replace it with a knowing that I am living as you lived. I don't want to keep score anymore. Jesus, change my heart. I don't want serving my spouse to be one more thing that I have to do today but instead to be one of the amazing things that I get to do today. I acknowledge that, in the past, this has been all about me and what I've done. My desire is to be more like you. I am a work in progress, putting my selfish desires in their proper place, behind those of my spouse. Jesus, you know my struggles in this area. Thank you for setting the example. Thank you for your willingness to demonstrate this fundamental truth for my marriage. Thank you that nothing was too dirty for you. Thank you that you served when everyone else was waiting for someone else to do it. No longer can I wait for my spouse to do what I think needs to be done. It's time for me to step into that role and just do it. Jesus, your example is overwhelming at times, and I thank you for your word that allows me to come back time and time again to learn more about how to live my life. Amen.

SECTION 6:

THERE IS HOPE

Hope is one of the most powerful words in the world. It holds promise. It speaks to the future. It is a lifeline. When you step out in your call to love your spouse, you are stepping into the hope of your future.

Hope comes from taking action. It happens when you get involved in the process. Jesus came with a message of hope. It is revealed time and time again as he spoke to those he encountered. With Jesus, it's not just the change that occurs at the moment but also the change that occurs over time.

DAY 36

Your Approach Makes All the Difference

"Come, follow me," Jesus said, "and I will send you out to fish for people." At once they left their nets and followed him.

MATTHEW 4:19-20

Jesus came with simple words and a simple attitude.

He did not demand.

He did not impose.

He did not threaten.

He did not issue ultimatums.

He did not lead with manipulation or coercion.

He did not lead with an iron fist.

He spoke to these men as equals.

He shared his vision.

He invited them.

We complicate things so much. We make our lives harder than they need to be. I have a hard time writing these words because when I look at how Jesus interacted with those around him, I am painfully aware that I do not always choose to treat Tony as Jesus would have. Many marriages, including ours, have had demands, manipulation, threats, ultimatums and ultimately heartache.

It will be this way!

We are doing this!

If you do that, I will _____.

This isn't the way that we are supposed to live our lives or our marriages. We've heard this Scripture before. We know this but have you ever stopped to think about the application to your marriage? There was no fight in Jesus' words to the disciples. This was not a battle to see things his way or to make them do something different. Choosing how we interact with our spouses is choosing whether or not hope will be a part of the equation.

Follow me...

I'm going this way, and I want you to come with me. Jesus didn't say that they had to follow him. He didn't say that he was going to make them follow him. He said, "Follow me. Come this way. Let's live this life." The disciples had options, they didn't have to follow Jesus. It was a choice that they made. It's the same choice that you have every day with your spouse. Do you want to go with them or will you head in the other direction?

Some days Tony and I are not headed in the same direction, and I'm sure that's true in your marriage too. Don't get hung up on all of those days, instead, try and see life from your spouse's perspective. Why? Because when Jesus said, "Follow me" it was an invitation to the disciples. Hope creates an invitation toward a new future. Where are the two of you going? In the case of the disciples it was to go where Jesus was leading, to be a part of that future that he was painting when he said...

and I will send you out to fish for people...

It's interesting that he was talking to fishermen when he said this because he didn't tell them that he was going to make them kings or doctors, things that they wouldn't have understood. Instead he said, "I will make you fishers of men." The disciples knew what fishing looked like, they understood the experience. They were able to grasp the concept, even though it wasn't fully explained to them how Jesus was going to have them fishing for men. I have to think that a few of them had puzzled looks on their faces, thinking "What does that even mean?" Jesus cast a vision and these men wanted to be a part of it even if they didn't fully understand the how or why.

I wonder if the vision in our marriages is as clear. I wonder if there are times when all my husband sees is me walking in circles. It's hard for someone to want to be a part of that. In order to lead others the vision has to be crystal clear to you. It was for Jesus. He knew that he was on a mission to gather men (and women), to stand in the gap for us and for our sins. What is the vision that you have for your marriage? Because Jesus knew his vision, he was able to share it and he created an environment where...

At once they left their nets and followed him.

At once. Immediately. Right now.

There wasn't any questioning. There wasn't any, "Let me think about this. Let me consider all of my options." Jesus was able to convey to these men that the future was better than what they currently were doing.

I know that in your marriage there has been times when one of you has said, "Wait, I

need all the facts." Or, "let's consider all of our options first." Or "I'm not sure." Every spouse has had a moment when you have doubted the leadership of the one that you are married to. It's human nature. It's allowing doubt and fear to creep into your marriage and rule over you instead of faith and freedom.

When your spouse is spending time with Jesus and is growing that relationship, there will be times when you need to put down what you are doing, even when it's something good, to follow, to go where your spouse is leading even when you don't have all the answers. It's exactly what the disciples did in the presence of Jesus.

It's time to lead in your marriage like Jesus led the disciples; quiet invitation, a vision cast and a response. Your marriage doesn't need to be a place of threats. It doesn't need to be a place of coercion or manipulation. It needs to be a place of vision, big vision. And you and your spouse need to respond to those invitations.

Stop putting up obstacles to the life that you were supposed to live.

Stop bringing negativity into a relationship that is supposed to foster growth.

Stop hurting each other with your words and actions.

Jesus led with a quiet powerful spirit. How much more could we accomplish if we were choosing to do life in this same way? If we chose this not just on our wedding day but every day of our marriage? It's time to start opening our eyes to the possibilities that exist instead of making excuses or coming up with why something won't work.

Jesus, thank you for the gift of simple words. Too many times I complicate things by speaking over and over again, going roundabout in circles. Holy Spirit, open my eyes to those times that I am not leading like Jesus, show me those times that I am trying to overpower my spouse to see things or do things my way. I don't want to lead with power but rather let me be aware of opportunities to lead with confidence. When my spouse is trying to lead me, let me look to them and the fruit of their lives to know when I just need to stop what I am doing and follow after them. I don't want my marriage to be one of blind following but rather of understanding that You make our paths straight and that leadership in you is leadership that we can not only believe in but confidently follow. Amen.

DAY 37:

What Are You Willing to Do for Love?

For God so loved the world that he gave his one and only Son, that whoever believes in him shall not perish but have eternal life.

JOHN 3:16

Love.

Limitless love.

Sacrificial love.

Unconditional love.

That is the love that you are to have for your spouse. God provides such a powerful example of true love in these 25 words. When God answered this question about YOU, he decided that you were so valuable that he would give his most cherished gift. He gave the one thing that was most important to him to show his love for you.

How much do you love your spouse?

Some of you are thinking, "It depends on the day or what they have done." Some of you are thinking, "I've never been more in love." Others are in a place where the answer is more, "I don't know right now." I often find that there are verses in the Bible that are transformational when I put my name in them...

For I so love Tony, that I would give...

Try it yourself.

For I so love my spouse _____, that I would give

_____.

What does this love look like to you? To the God of the universe, it was looking at humanity with such tremendous love that he was willing to give his only begotten Son, the Son in whom he was well pleased, so that you and I might have eternal life. God gave his ONLY, for the many. God choose to give that which mattered the most to him.

What matters the most to you?

Your phone.

Your job.

Your TV.

Your secrets.

Your baggage.

Your friends.

Your sports.

Your hobbies.

Your Facebook/Pinterest/Instagram time.

Your family.

I know in my own marriage that there have been many times when I haven't been willing to sacrifice what matters most to me to show my love to Tony. There have been many times when I have chosen to be selfish instead of selfless. When it has been my needs instead of his. Times when I have put limits on how much I would love him or how I would show that love. There have been times when I didn't want to sacrifice my comfort for the betterment of the relationship. I'm guessing that I am not the only one.

For God so loved the world that he gave...

Love and giving go hand in hand. This verse doesn't say that God so loved the world that he took or God so loved the world that he demanded. It says that God so loved the world that he gave. Marriage looks different when we choose to give, when we choose to sacrifice, when we remove the limits from the relationship. And yet, we are human and because of this I have to admit that in my marriage:

There are times when I react in anger.

There are times when I withhold affection.

There are times when I use harsh words.

There are times when I reject Tony.

There are times when I place blame on him instead of dealing with myself.

There are times when I don't even acknowledge this verse. Times when what I am calling love looks nothing like God's love.

Your marriage and mine need to be a place where God's love is seen and experienced. Not just something talked about.

It's not enough to say I love you.

God didn't just tell us that he loved us. He showed us. He showed us by willingly sacrificing his own child so that we could be drawn to him. I look over the list of things that have mattered more to me in my own marriage. I'm thinking of all of those times when I have allowed my actions to say I don't care about you or love you right now, I'm going to do my own thing. It's true what they say about the fact that the truth hurts. I have not always loved Tony the way that God loves me or in the way that God demonstrated his own love.

It's up to you and me to put our selfish desires aside for the health of our marriages. It's up to us to choose sacrificial, limitless love. God had a choice to make and so do we. God chose love and as result chose to sacrifice. You have that same choice in your marriage.

I know that there will be times when you choose selfishness, we are human after all.

However, when you are aware of how God demonstrated his love for you it makes it that much easier and desirable to show love in the same way to others. Love was never intended to burden you or to be an obligation. Loving someone has always been about the gift, the gift of your love.

God knew that we could never repay this gift, he wasn't waiting to see what gift we would give him in return. He simply gave, no strings attached, no expectations.

It's time to start loving our spouses in the same way. It's time to have more God in our marriages than "me". It's time to give the most valuable parts of you, of your time, of your resources, because of how God modeled this for you.

Jesus, thank you for demonstrating true love, powerful love, sacrificial, limitless love. I know that there have been many times when I have not acted in this same love toward my spouse, when I have chosen my needs over theirs. Times when it's been more important that I get what I want instead of what would be best for my spouse or for the relationship. The voice of the Holy Spirit is a powerful tool that you have given each one of us, the voice of correction, the voice of awareness. Make me more receptive to the prompting of the Holy Spirit. I want to be aware of the times when I am not showing love. I want to create an environment in my marriage where my spouse not only hears the words "I love you" but sees it in my actions and knows it in their heart. Enlarge my capacity to love someone besides myself. Enlarge my capacity to love someone that is imperfect, to love without expectation, to love with no strings attached. Jesus, equip me to love like YOU with a sacrificial love. Amen.

DAY 38:

Would You Climb a Tree?

Jesus entered Jericho and was passing through. A man was there by the name of Zacchaeus; he was a chief tax collector and was wealthy. He wanted to see who Jesus was, but because he was short he could not see over the crowd. So he ran ahead and climbed a sycamore-fig tree to see him, since Jesus was coming that way.

When Jesus reached the spot, he looked up and said to him, "Zacchaeus, come down immediately. I must stay at your house today." So he came down at once and welcomed him gladly.

All the people saw this and began to mutter, "He has gone to be the guest of a sinner."

But Zacchaeus stood up and said to the Lord, "Look, Lord! Here and now I give half of my possessions to the poor, and if I have cheated anybody out of anything, I will pay back four times the amount."

Jesus said to him, "Today salvation has come to this house, because this man, too, is a son of Abraham. For the Son of Man came to seek and to save the lost."

LUKE 19: 1-10

Zacchaeus a short, wealthy man who had the most hated profession of the day. He didn't have the size to be seen and he definitely didn't have the job that would have anyone welcoming him with open arms. He felt like he was on the outside looking in. He felt isolated and alone. He felt like many of you have felt in your marriage.

How often have you felt like God doesn't see you? In your marriage, how many times have you just hoped for a sighting of Jesus? If he would just look at our marriage...If I could just get a sense of

Jesus, I know that things would be better. Are you willing to go to the lengths that Zacchaeus did?

Here's a grown man, no matter how short he was, who willingly chose to climb a tree. Men did not do that in those days. I honestly can't even imagine too many men doing that today. It would be awkward. People might make fun. Who would take him seriously? He's the tax collector and he's climbing a tree? This is the person who made other's lives miserable and here he is acting like a child. What's he thinking?

He's thinking what you need to be thinking...I will do whatever it takes to be in Jesus' presence, to see him, to connect with him. I may have to take drastic steps to get Jesus into my marriage but it will be worth it, Jesus is worth it. Why? Because Jesus knows when you are making the time to get to know him better.

In this situation, Jesus immediately stops, looks at him and has a conversation in which he invites himself into Zacchaeus' house. Zacchaeus made a decision that he was going to take a big step to put himself in the presence of Jesus and Jesus met him right where he was. Did you know that it's that easy for you? Jesus wants to spend time with you. He wants to come to your house. He wants to be in all of your relationships, especially your marriage.

Are you seeking him and his involvement in your life? Are you willing to have Jesus come over and see what's going on? There are so many people who are willing to have Jesus in some areas of their life but not in other areas. They say, "Jesus, you can fix my finances or my kids, but I'll take care of the marriage or what happens in the bedroom." Jesus doesn't just want access to a few rooms in your house, he wants access to everything.

When Jesus starts talking to Zacchaeus, the tax collector immediately begins to repent for the mistakes that he has made. He doesn't wait for Jesus to start talking to him about his choices. He doesn't deny what he has done or try and minimize it. He admits to the cheating and stealing and talks about what he's going to do to fix things. You don't need other people pointing out what you have done wrong, the times that you have hurt your marriage or your spouse. You know the mistakes that you have made. The difference between most people and Zacchaeus comes in admitting and then taking action to make the situation right. Are you willing to own your responsibility for your actions?

So often, spouses want to downplay their mistakes and if it comes to correcting them, you only want to do the minimum. You want to do just enough to make it better but no more. Zacchaeus offers to fix things times 4. That's crazy! If he took $100 he was going to give back $400. He wasn't going to minimize his actions. He wasn't going to just meet the obligation he was going to go above and beyond. Where do you need to make things right in your marriage? Where do you need to offer more than what was taken? What actions do you need to take to not just repair the broken relationship but restore it to more than it was?

I love Jesus' closing words in the verse, "For the Son of Man came to seek and save the lost." The lost, not the folks that have it all together, not the ones who have no problems, not the ones who deny all of their faults. Jesus came to seek and save the lost, not the perfect. Do you know what this means? This means that Jesus came for you.

Jesus came for you, just like he came for Zacchaeus. Zacchaeus was lost in his actions, he was lost in his choices. Just like you, when you when you make a mistake in your marriage. Or when you when you say hurtful words. That's you when you try and hide your secrets. I am so thankful that Jesus came for the lost. I'm so thankful that one of the most hated people can receive the gift of salvation. I'm so thankful that Jesus saw Zacchaeus because that means that he sees you and me. I'm so thankful that in Jesus you have the opportunity to make your marriage right. That in him you have the strength and the ability to change.

Jesus, I am Zacchaeus. I am that short man that feels unseen and knows that I have made mistakes, that I have hurt others. Jesus, thank you for reminding me that you see me. I've lost sight of that truth so many times. I've felt invisible and alone and yet just like Zacchaeus, you see me. Jesus, I don't ever want to stop climbing that tree to be in your presence. Thank you for stopping to have a conversation with me and inviting yourself into my life. Thank you for the opportunity to acknowledge what I have done without condemnation and for the chance to make things right in my marriage. How powerful it is to know that with YOU, I have the ability to make things right. I know that I don't deserve this and I know that this is truly your grace. Let me step out in action to heal my marriage and to make things better than they were before. Amen.

DAY 39:

What Cross Do You Carry?

Then he said to them all: "Whoever wants to be my disciple must deny themselves and take up their cross daily and follow me. For whoever wants to save their life will lose it, but whoever loses their life for me will save it. What good is it for someone to gain the whole world, and yet lose or forfeit their very self?

LUKE 9:23-25

I don't like the first part of this verse. I don't want to be told to deny myself. I like what I have. I like being comfortable. I know that I am selfish. I know that there are times when I make life all about me. Times when I'm not focused on Tony or on our marriage. There are times when I make decisions in direct opposition to what is good for us.

Whoever wants to be my disciple must deny themselves and take up their cross daily and follow me

Not only is Jesus asking me to deny myself, he's then asking me to take up my cross daily. No one in that time carried a cross for fun. The one who carried the cross was the one who was going to hang on the cross. Think about the image of Jesus carrying the cross, his body beaten and broken, carrying this impossible weight that he knew was going to mean his death. He still chose to do it knowing all of this. He did it because you are so important that he willingly chose to deny who he was, and the power and authority that he has, in order that you would have eternal life.

I struggle with living like Jesus. I don't like being uncomfortable. I don't always want to do the hard things. I don't want to make the tough decisions all of the time. I want life to be easy. There have been many times in my marriage when I have "tried to save my life".

When I have tried to cover up poor decisions, when I haven't been completely (or even a little bit) truthful with Tony. When I have tried to minimize my actions to make me seem better. And yet Jesus words tell me that in these decisions, I lose my life.

What does that mean?

Losing my life means that I lose my integrity. It means that I lose my sense of self worth. It means that I lose the life that Jesus has in store for me when I try and do life my way, according to my plans instead of according to his word. It means that instead of bringing life to my marriage, I am destroying the life of marriage with these choices. I gain nothing.

I'll be the first to admit that in those split seconds my selfish decisions have felt like good ones, they have felt like they wouldn't hurt anyone. I have been able to rationalize that no one would ever know and yet I know…

I know when I have overspent and put us in financial jeopardy.

I know when I have kissed another man and compromised my wedding vows.

I know when I have lied and created a web of deceit and broken trust.

I know when I have spoken poorly of Tony and allowed others to think less of him.

I know when I have damaged my marriage.

In each of these instances and in many more, I have willingly traded a piece of myself for the pleasures of the world. I have traded my vows for temporary fixes. None of which have mattered in the long run. In saving my life, I have, in every instance, sacrificed my marriage.

How amazing is it that in his perfect love, Jesus gives us the remedy. Have you noticed that throughout the words of Jesus, he never leaves us with a problem that doesn't have a solution? There is always a way if we are willing to take it.

...whoever loses their life for me will save it...

What does it mean for me to lose my life, especially after I have already had to deny myself and take up my cross? That sounds like a lousy way to live. It doesn't sound like any fun. It's in such direct opposition to the way that the world sees marriage that it's a struggle for most and yet here it is in the Bible.

The world tells you that your happiness, your satisfaction, is the most important thing that you can do for yourself. It's all about you. If you're not happy change your partner, your job, your life. The world tells you that if you aren't happy you need to change the external circumstances. Jesus doesn't deal so much with the external as he does with the internal.

When you lose your life for Jesus, it's a willingness to lose the lies. It's a choice to lose the deception. It's a decision to live life without selfishness, to put others first. All of the things that we think make our life a little easier. These are the things that Jesus is saying no to. These are the things that are destroying your marriage and mine.

It's time for you to live the marriage that God intended for you.

It's time for you to live the life that Jesus intended for you.

It's time to get your life back.

It's exhausting to live for the world. The world is constantly changing the rules. The world is constantly changing trends. You never know from one day to the next what is acceptable.

Yet, if today, you decide to give your life to Jesus, to live for him and according to him, today is the day that everything changes. You don't have to be exhausted in your life. You don't have to be exhausted in your marriage. It's as simple as asking Jesus to come in, asking him to take over, asking him to show you what needs to be done and then doing it. What seems hard in the beginning becomes easier the more that you do it.

Are you ready?

Are you ready to stop fighting the uphill battle?

Are you ready to stop losing yourself in this world?

Jesus, I have made so many mistakes trying to live in the world and trying to live by the world's rule. I have become confused and lost. I have hurt so many people especially my spouse. I know that I can't do it by myself anymore, no matter how hard I try. Jesus, come into my life. I want you here. I want you to be my Lord and Savior. I want you to be the Lord and Savior of my marriage. I am so thankful that you are a God that would never ask me to do something that you, yourself have not done. I don't want to do marriage the way that I have been doing it. You know it hasn't worked that way. Thank you for being patient with me. Thank you for giving me an opportunity for a do over. Today, I invite you into my life and into my marriage. Open my eyes to the ways that I can become more like you toward my spouse. Amen.

DAY 40:

The Ultimate Act of Service

For even the Son of Man did not come to be served, but to serve, and to give His life a ransom for many."

MARK 10:45

The Son of Man, the Messiah, God Most High, King...Jesus, did not come to be served but to serve. Jesus' first task and really the only task here on earth was to serve others. From his earliest encounters with people he was serving them through teaching, he served in creating community, he gave to others in the miracles.

As the Son of God, he could have demanded to be treated like a king. He could have expected certain behavior from others. He could have thrown a fit when the folks in his hometown didn't recognize who he was or what he had been sent to do. Instead we are reminded that being served was never the goal. It was always to serve.

I wish that I could say the same. I wish that I could say that has always been my goal in my marriage but I would be lying. There have been many times, more than I wish to count, when my attitude with Tony has been serve ME. Take care of MY needs. Do this for ME.

I think if you are honest with yourself you can see those times in your marriage too. Those times when you didn't want to serve your spouse. Those times when you could have served him or her but instead turned the tables and made it all about you.

If only you could see my face right now. It's marked by sadness. I'm sad for all of the opportunities that I forfeited the chance to be Jesus to Tony. I'm sad for all of the times that I made it about me, when it should have been about him or about us. I'm sad that my actions have over the years had a ripple effect in our home and in our community.

When we insist on being served, when our selfishness rears it's ugly head and becomes the focus in our marriage, it's not just us that suffers. Your spouse suffers as they question their value and desirability. Your family suffers as kids learn from watching. Every time it becomes about YOU, your kids are learning how to make it about them. Your community suffers when another marriage starts to crumble because of selfishness. Our world suffers because every broken marriage, leads to more brokenness and pain in the world. The insistence on only being served in your marriage impacts the entire world, starting inside of your home.

Here's the good news. You don't have to keep acting like that. Jesus gives us the antidote to our selfishness in these words, "The Son of Man...came to serve."

That's it.

Jesus came to serve. It's that simple and that hard all at the same time. Serve. How can you serve your spouse? How can you make it more about them and less about you. Now, I know that some of you reading this right now are saying, "Alisa, I serve my spouse all of the time, what about me? What about them serving me? When are they going to do that?"

I hear you. I also know that you are the one reading this book right now and not them. You cannot change a person BUT you can change your environment. Start with yourself and your heart as you let God take care of changing them.

Find opportunities to serve not out of obligation, not so you can keep score, not so you can remind them of it 100 times. Find opportunities to serve because that is what Jesus did. You and I have no better role model. We have no better example of how to do life. No movie star, super model or reality TV star will ever compare to the role model that we have in Jesus.

There is nothing to be gained in demanding to be served. It creates an environment of hostility and resentment. It creates an environment in which relationships wither and die. It's an environment where people give up and check out. Demanding to be served takes love out of the equation and replaces it with duty and avoidance. Not the best recipe for a happy marriage.

What happens to you and to your marriage when you adopt the attitude of Jesus? When you come with understanding that you will serve? First let me say, that in Jesus' service he was not a doormat. He did not let people walk all over him. Sometimes people equate service with being subservient and that's not Jesus' model.

When I approach Tony with an attitude of serving, I come with a willingness to understand his needs, I come with a desire to put my selfishness to the side for his desires. This can be the biggest shift in a marriage. When you choose to serve your spouse with no expectation of anything in return, you gift them the opportunity to be loved in the place that they are, as they are. Each of us longs for acceptance, we long to be valued. Serving demonstrates both of those.

Jesus, I don't know if I would have made the same decisions that you did in coming to earth. Honestly, I think that I would have used the God card at least once or twice just to see what I could get. Thank you for not being me. Thank you for being an example of what service looks like EVEN WHEN you could demand to be served. I know that there have been times in my marriage when I have demanded that my spouse serve me. I know that because of this I have damaged my marriage. Jesus, I pray for healing in my relationship. I pray that when I see opportunities to serve I do not shy away from them but walk boldly into them, walk boldly into loving on my spouse the way that you have taught me. I don't want to use the role models in this world as an example of how to love selfishly. Rather I choose you and choose the way that you love as my model. Amen.

ACKNOWLEDGMENTS

As I sit here at the end of this journey, I realize that there are so many people who have had a hand in crafting this book. An author is the one who writes the words but that can only happen in an environment of support and I am blessed to have one of the best. To all of you, thank you from the bottom of my heart.

For every coaching client who has trusted me with their relationship, thank you! It is no small task to be vulnerable to another person and I am honored that so many around the world have allowed me to walk alongside their journey of healing and restoration.

Jurgen and Leanne Matthesius, thank you for the step of faith that you took in coming to San Diego all those years ago. Your journey intersected with mine at a God appointed time and I am so appreciative of the ability to continuously learn from you.

Colin, Melissa, and all the members of our Connect Group, you are family and words cannot describe how much you mean to me. The words of life you speak have transformed who I am. I am forever grateful for every hug, smile and laugh we share.

Cori and Theresa, every 2 weeks for the last 3 years we have met to discuss business and life. You <u>always</u> ask me about my goals, listen to my fears and remind me that I <u>can</u> do this.

Courtney and Crystal, thank you for the heartfelt conversations at Starbucks. You lovingly pushed me out of my comfort zone and held me accountable.

Rosanna and Elise, you created an amazing group for entrepreneurial women to encourage one another and share our successes and challenges. Because of this step that you took, I have been stretched in ways never imagined.

Christi, Jennie and Chelsie, thank you for texting me, praying for me, and smiling, when once again, I was talking about Called to Love. It's on to the next one now!

Morgan, you took my words and thoughts and crafted them into a cover that is more than just a cover, it's a picture of the hope contained in these pages.

Cori, you make me look amazing every time I get in front of your camera. You make it easy to smile.

For every friend who has listened to the story of this book, who has asked how it it going, who has said, "I can't wait to read it!" Thank you for being a cheerleader. The world needs the encouragement that you bring.

Beth & Lu, Carmen & Vincie, thank you for heeding the call to love in your own marriage and for being an example for what this type of love looks like. I am honored to be your daughter.

Alex and Abby, thank you for putting up with me when I was distracted with writing this book, when I was sitting at the coffee shop when you woke up, when I was tired from writing. I thank God, that I was called to love you as my children.

Tony, I have loved you for such a long time. More importantly you have loved me. You have loved me with a love that I don't deserve. Thank you for being more than I could have ever dreamed when I said YES all those years ago. Thank you for answering the call to love over and over again in our marriage.

Jesus, thank you for showing us all what it truly means to love.

Alisa DiLorenzo is a sought-after international marriage coach, speaker, a best-selling author, and the co-host of the ONE Extraordinary Marriage Show, which is downloaded in 180 countries. The author of The Trust Factor, Connect Like You Did When You First Met, and 7 Days of Sex Challenge are in the hands of couples worldwide. She and her husband, Tony, have two kids and live in San Diego. Learn more at OneExtraordinaryMarriage.com

STAY ENGAGED

with Called to Love and Alisa DiLorenzo

#CalledToLove

CalledToLoveBook.com

CONNECT

with Alisa DiLorenzo

BOOKS BY ALISA

Stripped Down: 13 Keys to Unlocking the Intimacy In Your Marriage

7 Days of Sex Challenge: How To Rock Your Sex Life and Your Marriage

Connect Like You Did When You First Met: 101 Proven Questions for Couples

The Trust Factor: How To Rebuild Trust In Your Marriage

extraordinary marriage

ONE Extraordinary Marriage was founded by Tony and Alisa DiLorenzo in 2009. ONE Extraordinary Marriage was created to provide couples with the tools, resources, and strategies to overcome their intimacy challenges. We understand that it takes work... hard work and transparency to get back the intimacy once shared between two committed people. We understand because we've been there. Our process is for real couples experiencing real problems. We tackle the tough stuff and candidly discuss all aspects of a marriage, including sex. Do you remember what it feels like to be deeply in love, to have a deep rooted connection? ONE Extraordinary Marriage can help you achieve that and more.

Call: 858-848-7132

Email: Support@OneExtarordinaryMarriage.com

Visit us online at: OneExtrarodinaryMarriage.com

Made in the USA
Middletown, DE
09 June 2017